Dump Debt & Build Bank

The Everyday Chick's Guide to Money

Faneisha D.R. Alexander

To get the most out of this book, access the accompanying Everyday Chick's Guide to Money digital workbook by visiting ***girltalkwithfo.teachable.com***

ISBN: 978-1-796904-46-8

Disclaimer:

This publication is designed to provide accurate and authoritative information with regard to the subject matter covered. It is sold with the understanding that neither the author nor publisher is engaged in rendering legal, financial, accounting, or other professional advice by publishing this book. If financial advice or other expert assistance is required, the services of a competent professional should be sought. The author and publisher disclaim any liability, loss, or risk incurred as an outcome, directly or indirectly, through the use and application of any contents of this work.

Visit the website at *www.GirlTalkwithFo.com*

Editor: Andrea Jasmin | ACJasminProofreading.com

Proofreader: Erica Wilkerson

ISBN: 978-1-796904-46-8

DEDICATION

This book is dedicated to the women chasing their dreams and building a legacy.

To those who want better for their future and for their family.

You can create the life that you want, one decision at a time.

To my Dad. I know you're proud. Cheers to a second one under my belt! I imagine you smiling from ear to ear.

To my husband, Ben. I love you. Thank you for your support of my many dreams—including this one.

To my family—this legacy is for you!

CONTENTS

ACKNOWLEDGMENTS

There is absolutely no way that I would be able to do this without the help of these amazing people. I'm abundantly thankful to:

Ben Alexander, my husband. You supported the vision and gave me the space to create. Thanks for holding down the fort while I labored to complete this work.

Andrea Jasmin, my editor. You didn't think it robbery to put in the extra hours and care to help bring this dream to life in weeks! Thanks for grabbing hold of my wild idea and pushing me to the finish line.

Erica Wilkerson, my best friend. You literally save the day every single time! Thanks for always helping me put my best foot forward.

The Girl Talk with Fo VIP Squad. I wrote this book with you in mind. Thanks for being my cheerleaders and the reason that I continue to do what I do. You're the real MVPs.

INTRODUCTION

At this point in my life, I was fed up. I was trying to get my financial life together, but it seemed like I kept hitting a wall.

I had already been declined for the credit card that was supposed to help me improve my credit score and I had paid my financial "advisor"— and I use the term advisor loosely— $600, only to be left in a worse position than I was before.

If he couldn't help me, then I knew I was on my own.

I scoured the Internet for articles and books that could just help me get on the right track, but none of the books that I found were making sense or even related to me.

I wasn't out here drinking lattes every day, buying designer clothes, trying to be the black version of Carrie Bradshaw. I just wanted to get out of debt, be able to put some money in savings, and not live paycheck to paycheck.

Was that too much to ask?

Apparently it was, because no one seemed to get it! Where were the personal finance books to help people like me? Where were the money tips for the everyday chick?

My Money Story

By the time I graduated college (again) in 2011, I found myself in over $78,000 of student loan debt and little to no savings.

I had done all of the "right" things, yet I still found myself in this situation.

Go to college. *Check*
Go *back* to college. *Check*
Get an internship. *Check*
Get a decent job with a stable company. *Check*
Excel in said job. *Check*

Amidst all of those checks, I had apparently x-ed out on finances. *Was it one of the classes that I missed in undergrad?*

I watched, miserably, as my former classmates were traveling the world, wondering why I didn't have the finances to do the same, even with a "good job."

Really, how could someone with two degrees in engineering not be able to manage money? It is math after all.

Maybe I was making this money thing more complicated than it needed to be.

Reality set in that I could be spending the next 30 years of my life paying off the debt that I had accrued to get those degrees. I didn't even like my major, so the thought of being reminded of it every month was excruciating.

I had replayed the should've, could've, would'ves in my head so many times at this point.

I should've applied for more scholarships. I could've worked more during school. Had I known the amount of debt that I would accumulate, I wouldn't have gone to graduate school.

Trust me. I thought of every possible scenario for what could have kept me out of debt, but knew that I couldn't change anything. This was my reality that I had to face. It was time to put on my big girl undies and get to work.

My Wake Up Call

I remember sitting in a church service listening as the pastor walked us through his personal finance series. He was talking about living within the margins—using a sheet of paper as his visual reference.

In a gist, he showed us how we should be sowing, saving, and spending our money appropriately.

During one of his messages, he had families come to the front of the church to share their testimonies for getting out of debt and living in financial peace.

There was one family whose story I remember specifically.

I sat in the back of the church—obviously late—as a single mother of two young boys shared how she was completely debt free—home included.

I thought, *"How nice. Good for them!"* not really understanding the magnitude of what this woman had just done. I didn't have a mortgage, after all. I was just sitting there buried in my "little" student loan debt.

The pastor went on to challenge us to sell unused items in our homes to put toward paying off debt. He also encouraged us to sign up for Financial Peace University—a course that was being held at the church.

I didn't sign up, but I kept that story tucked away in my memory.

A year later, I found myself packing up and moving back across the country to South Carolina.

After a few months in, I connected with an old classmate from college to catch up. Soon after, we started dating.

During one of our couch conversations, we started talking about finances. To be honest, I'm not sure how the discussion started, but at the end of it, I learned that my then boyfriend was completely debt free and had paid cash for both of his vehicles.

This was unheard of. *Was I dating an alien?*

Outside of the woman's story that I had heard at church, I didn't know anyone who was debt free, let alone paying for cars in cash. *What was this sorcery?*

He asked if I had heard of Dave Ramsey and the book, *The Total Money Makeover*.

Dave Ramsey . . . Dave Ramsey . . . Dave Ramsey . . . Oh yea, the guy who developed the Financial Peace University course that I had opted out of just a year prior. That Dave Ramsey.

"Yes, of course I know who Dave Ramsey is," I responded.

I shared the story of the single mom who was debt free with him and decided to pick up the book.

Prior to this point, I had already tried a financial advisor and truly wanted to get my finances together. If this book could do that for him, I was willing to give it a shot.

I read the book in about three days and after finishing it, I immediately cleared my savings account down to $1,000 and started paying off my debt.

It hurt. *Did Dave not know how long it took me to save $1,000 while broke?* I mean it took years of birthday and Christmas cards to scrounge up money for my savings and it was gone within mere seconds.

A year and one month later, I had paid off all of my undergraduate student loans— $24,000. Two years after that, I not only cash flowed my wedding, but I was completely debt free.

So how exactly did I go from living paycheck to paycheck to becoming debt free with a multi-six figure net worth?

I'm glad you asked.

My purpose for writing this book is to share the money lessons that I learned along my own journey. This is the book that I wish was written for people like me when I needed it. My goal is that this book becomes the ultimate money manual for the everyday woman who wants to get control of her finances and stop living paycheck to paycheck.

In this book, I walk you through getting out of debt, managing your finances, and building wealth in an easy to understand and relatable way. I take the fluff (and hard to understand words) out of personal finance and give you exactly what you need to start making changes in your finances today.

In the first section of the book, *First Things First*, I lay the foundation for the mindset shift that has to take place if you want to change the course of your finances. Without the right mindset, none of the practical tips that I share in this book will matter. We'll identify what your conceptions of money are and how your upbringing has shaped that. You'll learn to reprogram your mind to operate in abundance and wealth.

We have a tendency to skip the mindset work, so I'm telling you in advance not to do this. The first part of this book is the most critical. Many times, we are not hindered by our inability to do the work. Instead, we're held back by poor and limiting mindsets that keep us in cycles of bad financial decisions.

Do the mindset work first and then you'll have the proper grounding to begin doing the tactical work.

Next, we'll dive into the *Dump Your Debt*, section of the book. In this section, I share tried and true methods for getting out of debt quickly. Don't skip straight to this part. Trust me, if your mind isn't right, the work that you do in this section will not stick.

I share more details about my debt free journey and provide the hacks that helped me pay off debt quickly. You'll find that anyone—at any income level—can pay off debt with the steps that I share.

After we work through getting out of debt, it's time to *Build Your Bank*. I don't know about you, but I love making money. Maybe I was born with a money making gene, but I have a knack for turning ideas into money.

If you're like me, then you'll enjoy the jewels that I share in this section. I walk you through maximizing the current income that you receive from your 9 to 5 job, how to earn more, how to create additional streams of income, and how to build a profitable business.

Lastly, I'll talk about leaving a legacy. Getting out of debt, making tons of money, and building wealth isn't just for you. The goal isn't just to have money for the sake of having it. Your financial journey is for you *and* your legacy.

I teach you how to make these financial changes in your life stick and last for generations to come.

At the conclusion of this book you will be equipped with the tools and resources necessary to dump debt, build bank, and create the life that you want.

Let's get started.

Section 1: First Things First

CHAPTER 1: SHIFT YOUR MONEY MINDSET

Before I get into the practical steps that you can use to master your money, I have to first address the true root of winning with money—your mindset.

There aren't any statistics to prove it, but I believe that mastering money is 99% mindset and 1% math. At least, it's been the case in my experience.

We all have our own beliefs about money. Whether we knew it or not, that belief was embedded in us as a child. It was shaped by what we saw and experienced when it came to money.

Those raised in poverty may have grown up believing that money was the ticket to escaping the economic fate of their parents, while those raised in affluence may view money as an easily accessible commodity of which they can attain quickly and spend frivolously.

Our life's experience has shaped what we think of money.

At a young age I knew that I never wanted to fret about money. I had seen enough to know that I always wanted to have it and I never wanted to spend it.

Every time I'd get any money from birthdays or holidays, I'd stuff it in an envelope that I had taped to the back of my headboard so that I wouldn't spend it or lose it.

It didn't take long for my parents to catch on to my seemingly frugal nature. I quickly became labeled as the tight fist of the family, while simultaneously being told that I'd one day be a millionaire because of it. Little did they know that they were merely prophesying over my life.

That mindset of never wanting to be stressed about money followed me through adulthood. So, to wake up one day and find myself living paycheck to paycheck completely devastated me.

How did I let this happen?

I immediately felt like a failure. Fortunately, I at least knew one thing about failure— it isn't final until you don't get up.

Over the course of nearly three years and paying off $78,000 in debt, I began shifting my mindset around money and my relationship with it.

I had to release the notion of being a failure with my money, while also removing the fear of lack of resources for my life. I had to learn that money isn't to be hoarded to hedge against seemingly inevitable bad times, but that it is a tool to be used to make our lives and the world a better place.

So, before we begin, I want you to also shift your mindset on money.

Take a moment to reflect on the things that you learned about money as a child by answering the following questions:

How did your parent(s) handle money growing up?

Did you experience financial lack or abundance?

How did what you saw or experienced shape your relationship with money?

Do you identify with any of these limiting mindsets?

- ❑ Money is scarce
- ❑ Debt is a part of life
- ❑ You have to be good at math to master money
- ❑ Wealth is only inherited
- ❑ More money, more problems
- ❑ Poverty is equivalent to being humble
- ❑ You must work all of your life

In order for the tips shared in this book to work for you, you must begin by dismissing any limiting beliefs that you have about money in exchange for the following truths.

Truth 1: Money Can Be Mastered

The phrase that I hear all too often is, *"I'm bad with money."*

Several years ago, I read the book *The Tongue: A Creative Force by Charles Capps*. It was a book given to my father as he battled pancreatic cancer—in hopes that he would learn the Biblical principle of using words to shift, change, and create circumstances in our lives. After stumbling upon it years later, I decided to read it for myself.

Despite hearing the adage, *"Words have power"* for years, this book truly opened my eyes to just how much power is in our words.

I immediately began to apply the principles of the book to my finances. Removing phrases like, "I'm broke," from my vocabulary. After fully understanding the power of words, I was no longer going to speak lack of money into my life.

So, when I hear the phrase, *"I'm bad with money,"* I immediately cringe, because the person saying it has no idea what they just did to their finances.

Speaking a declarative statement like that means you have already convinced yourself, decided, and believe in your mind that you cannot master money. You've handicapped your mind from coming up with solutions or resources to handling money more effectively. And, unless you begin changing those words and thoughts, you've just sentenced yourself to a life of financial lack and poor financial decisions.

Let's cancel that belief right now!

Say this out loud: *"I will master money!"*

Repeat it over and over again. I want you to repeat it until you believe it, because the notion that you can't master money is false!

I believe that many people think that they can't master money because they've been trying to manage it without being taught how.

Imagine being put on a job with no training and being asked to produce at the highest level. It seems impossible and it's certainly frustrating, right? Money is no different. We're thrust into adulthood without even being taught how to budget, yet we're expected to flourish in our finances.

But here's the good news: It's never too late to be taught!

So, say it out loud one more time: *I will master money!*

Truth 2: Money Is The Tool, Not The Treasure

Think back to the first time that you said you wanted to be a millionaire.

If I'm accurate, you were probably a young kid missing your two front teeth and instead of saying "millionaire," you said something more like "gubazillionaire!"

Fast forward to your teenage years and I'm sure you were sorely disappointed when you got "S" for shack in the game of MASH.

Now that you're an adult, I'm sure that desire to be wealthy hasn't changed. Afterall, I don't know of many people in their right mind who want to be poor or live paycheck to paycheck. I believe that the sheer fact that we can imagine and dream such impossible numbers like "gubazillionaire" as children is a testament to the certitude that we're inherently created to prosper.

God created us to be wealthy, but not just for the sake of having money. Instead, our money is to be used to provide access and opportunity.

Money is the tool, not the treasure.

Having money isn't the end goal; the opportunities and access that money can afford you is really the treasure.

We all want to be able to afford better opportunities and experiences for our life and our family's lives. No one wants to have money just to look at it in the bank.

Here's what money really is:

Money is *a debt free college education*
Money is *being able to travel the world*
Money is *experiencing luxury*
Money is *helping someone in need*
Money is *building shelters for the homeless*
Money is *paying for a single mom's groceries because you know what it's like to struggle*

Money is *gifting a college scholarship to a kid who can't afford to go*
Money is being *free to do the work that God has called you to do on earth*

Money is the tool and not the treasure and this is too often misunderstood.

Take a moment to answer the following questions:

- ★ What would you do if you were completely debt free?
- ★ What is your motivation for wanting more money in your life?
- ★ What could more money afford you and your family?

Ultimately, your desire to be better in your finances and to attain wealth should have a purpose. What is that purpose? Figure it out and that will be the motivation for you mastering money.

TRUTH 3: MONEY IS MAGNETIC

Have you ever noticed that people who are wealthy always seem to get more money, while people who struggle with money rarely get more?

Though the wealthy are applying some of the multiplication principles that we'll discuss later in the book, there's one universal law that's always on their side. That law? Money goes to and stays with those who manage it well.

In essence, money is attracted to those who treat it right. And like people, it'll always stay where it's being treated well. Therefore, being a good money manager makes you a magnet for money.

This principle was at work in The Parable of the Talents found in the Bible. The servants who managed their talents well were given more, while the one who did not was cast out and his portion was given to the one with the most.

"... You have been faithful in handling this small amount, so now I will give you many more responsibilities ..." Matthew 25:21, NLT

When you begin applying the tips shared in this book, you will begin to see this law at work in your life. The more that you become faithful and responsible with your money, the more you will see money come to you.

Say this out loud: *"I am a money magnet because I am a money manager!"*

Throughout this book, I will provide more truths that will continue to shift and elevate your money mindset. I'll challenge deeply embedded beliefs about money that will allow you to break free from the bondage of debt and lack of finances into a life of financial freedom and abundance.

Are you ready?

✎ *Action:* I've included 20 affirmations around money, many of which I repeat daily. Read them. Remember them. Recite them. Receive them.

---

20 Money Affirmations To Repeat Daily

1. I will master money.
2. I am a money magnet because I am a money manager.
3. I generate multi-million-dollar ideas.
4. I lack nothing.
5. Money comes to me because I walk in purpose.
6. Resources are attracted to me.
7. I have the wisdom to manage money.
8. Money flows to me with ease and abundance.
9. I owe no man nothing but love.
10. I am prosperous.
11. I am the lender and not the borrower.
12. I renounce poverty thinking.
13. I am wealthy with ideas and, therefore money.
14. Money comes to me in unexpected ways.
15. My finances are in order.
16. I am the master of my money and my money does not master me.
17. I use money as a tool and not as a treasure.
18. I have access to an unlimited source of ideas and money.
19. I live in overflow and abundance.
20. Money comes to me with ease and in abundance.

Section 2: Dump Your Debt

Chapter 2: Know What You Owe

The first time that I actually realized how much debt I was in, I was devastated. I honestly had no idea how much I had borrowed (with interest) for the two degrees that I don't even use today.

I enrolled into college at 17 years old. I was so excited about finally being in college that I was completely clueless on what my stay was actually costing me. I had received some small scholarships for academics, but was rejected for financial aid. My parents did what they could reasonably do after having just paid for my sister's private college tuition. What they didn't cover was picked up by student loans.

The parentals made one thing unequivocally clear: Graduate in 4 years! Looking back, I realized why. Seven straight years of having your income go to college tuition is not the business!

I heeded their advice and finished in 4 years, plus summer school sessions. Immediately following graduation, I enrolled in graduate school because, quite frankly, I wasn't ready to be an adult.

This time though, I was a bit more aware of the price of my education.

The sticker price for my one-year graduate school program was $54,000. I remember because I was literally blown away by the fact that one year could cost more than my four years of undergrad.

I mean, was the diploma going to be laced in gold, diamonds, and glitter? If anything, it'd better at least guarantee me a high paying job!

I kept telling myself that I would be going to Duke University. I grew up as a basketball junkie, so it was a lifelong dream of mine to attend the college basketball capital of America. But when I saw the price I second guessed enrolling.

My mom encouraged me to take the (seemingly) once in a lifetime opportunity and I did.

A year later I graduated—job in hand, but debt repayment ensuing.

While in school, I was introduced to this new website that helped you manage money by connecting each of your financial accounts. The website, Mint.com, is still active today and is one that I would recommend for those who are ok with having your financial data consolidated into one place online.

I signed up for a free profile and started linking my accounts to it. Taking everything into consideration, the site was able to calculate my net worth.

Net worth - A measure of financial worth calculated by subtracting your liabilities (debts) from your assets (things you own that have financial value.)

Net Worth = Assets - Liabilities

My net worth was in the NEG-A-TIVE, and not just by a little bit! I had little to no assets—which at the time was only the money in my bank account—and *over* $78,000 in student loan debt.

Despite the depressing reality of it all though, it was the wake up call that I needed to do SOMETHING.

As daunting and scary as it may seem, you have to know what you owe. Using Mint.com allowed me to have a full picture of what I owed and to whom.

Do you know the total amount of debt that you owe? Down to the penny amount?

As you're making minimum payments to different loan companies, the total debt that you owe sometimes escapes you. You're so focused on making the payment that you're not even aware of what your overall debt is. Knowing what you owe in total is critical to creating a plan to pay it off.

Ignorance is *not* bliss, especially when it comes to your finances.

The first step to making any change in your life—be it finances, health, or even your career—is knowing where you are now. You have to know where you are now to create a plan for where you want to be.

What You Need To Know

Just knowing your balance isn't enough, though. There are a few things that you need to understand about your debt so that you can effectively tackle it.

Principal Balance

Your principal balance is the amount that you've actually borrowed or, as the name implies, the "main" balance. Though this is the amount that you've borrowed, it is typically not the final amount that you will pay back. Lenders will apply interest to this balance, which will be added to calculate the total amount due.

Interest Rate

Interest rate is a percentage of your principal balance that is charged for use of the funds and is typically given as an annual rate.

This number is important because it allows you to calculate what the actual cost of your debt is in total. To calculate the total cost, or new balance, of a principal loan, you'd use the following equation:

$$Balance\ Due = Principal\ Balance * (1 + Interest\ Rate\ as\ Decimal)$$

I'll use this calculation to show what the total cost of a $1,000 credit card balance is at a 24% annual interest rate.

$$Balance\ Due = \$1,000 * (1 + .24)$$

$$Balance\ Due = \$1,240$$

In this scenario, it would cost you an additional $240 in interest to borrow $1,000.

Though this is a good visual to show how interest works and is applied to your balance, very rarely is interest this straight forward. Instead, most lenders use what is called compound interest.

Compound Interest

Compound interest is interest applied to already accumulated interest on a principal balance.

Compound interest is often lauded as the 8th wonder of the world because of its ability to quickly multiply money; however, as a borrower, it is your worst nightmare! It can quickly take a $1,000 loan and turn it into a $3,000 loan.

Let's go back to our $1,000 loan example.

Imagine that you take out this loan and don't make any payments for 5 years. Barring your debt goes into collections and other fees are applied, here's what your balance would look like with compound interest after 5 years:

Year	Balance	Interest	New Balance with Compound Interest	New Balance with Regular Interest
1	$1,000	24%	$1,240	$1,240
2	$1,240	24%	$1,538	$1,480
3	$1,538	24%	$1,907	$1,720
4	$1,907	24%	$2,364	$1,960
5	$2,364	24%	$2,932	$2,200

As you can see, with the wonder of compound interest, you'll pay $732 more in interest over the same time period than if the interest were just calculated from your principal balance of $1,000.

This example assumed that the interest on the balance was only compounded annually; however, most lenders compound monthly, or even as much as daily.

Compound Frequency

The frequency at which you are charged interest on your balance is referred to as your compound frequency. It is the number of time periods that your annual interest rate will be spread across.

Now, I'll admit that calculating your compounded interest (accumulated interest over a certain period) is a trickier equation, but I'll attempt to make it easier for you.

If your compound frequency is one month—meaning, each month interest is applied to your accumulated debt—you would need to know what the equivalent interest rate is for one month as opposed to a year. To do this, you'd just divide your yearly interest rate by 12 months.

$$Monthly\ Compounded\ Interest\ Rate = \frac{Annual\ Interest\ Rate}{12\ months}$$

In the case of the $1,000 loan, the monthly compounded interest rate would be:

$$\frac{24\%\ per\ year}{12\ months} = .02\ (or\ 2\%)$$

Based on this calculation, you would be charged 2% of your ending balance each month.

Likewise, if your interest is compounded daily, you could just divide your monthly interest rate by 30 or 31 days. Your lender will specify the number of days within a billing cycle.

In our example, the daily interest rate would be:

$$\frac{2\%\ per\ month}{31\ days} = .000645\ (or\ .0645\%)$$

Knowing the frequency at which your interest is compounded allows you to calculate exactly how much interest is accumulating during a specified time period. This is important because you'll be able to see exactly how much of your payment will go toward interest and what will go toward your principal balance.

You'll find that often the minimum payment typically only covers the total interest that has accumulated.

Minimum Payment

The minimum payment is the minimum amount that you can pay on your debt to avoid your account going into default or being sold to collections.
Though paying the minimum may seem like a viable strategy for saving money, it is not a great long-term decision.

By your lender's design, the minimum payment is typically enough to cover the accumulated interested on your balance with a few dollars left to apply to the principal balance. This means that it will take years to actually reduce the principal balance that you owe, and eventually, pay off your debt.

Your lenders understand that the longer they can keep your monthly balance high, the more interest they'll be able to make from the loan. Simply put, the longer they can keep you in debt, the more money they can make. That's the name of the game.

Paying more than the minimum balance is necessary to getting out of debt. I'll share more on ways that you can do so in the subsequent sections.

Let's revisit the $1,000 loan example one more time to demonstrate the trap of minimum payments.

For this portion of the example, we'll assume that your interest is compounded monthly at a rate of 2% and your minimum payment is $22. In some cases, the lender will subtract your payment from the balance before applying interest—I'll do the same.

Month	Balance	Minimum Payment	New Balance	Monthly Interest	Ending Balance
1	$1,000	$22	$978	2%	$998
2	$998	$22	$976	2%	$996
3	$996	$22	$974	2%	$993
4	$993	$22	$971	2%	$990
5	$990	$22	$968	2%	$987
6	$987	$22	$965	2%	$984

After six months and a total of $132 paid, the balance on this loan only decreased by $16. A mere 12% of the total payments made actually went to the principal balance!

If I were to continue this exercise you'd see that it would take 9 years of making the minimum payment to pay off this loan. The total amount paid? Nearly $2,500!

Are you seeing how the game is played now?

Only paying the minimum balance on your debt will keep you in debt much longer than you need to be and it will cost you way more than you intended on paying. Remember, debt is a trap.

Where To Go To Find Out What You Owe

The primary place that you need to go to find out what you owe is your lender. Though credit score tracking sites, like Credit Karma, or even sites like Mint.com pull in your information, it's not always up to date.

To ensure that you have accurate, up-to-date info, you need to go directly to your lender via their website or by requesting information by phone.

You'll not only want to get your current balance, interest rate, and compound frequency, but it'll also be useful to get your payment history. Your payment history will show exactly how much of your payments have actually been going to your principal balance.

The more information that you have, the better plan that you'll be able to make to attack your debt.

✎ *Action:* Complete the **Know What You Owe** worksheet that can be found in the Everyday Chick's Guide to Money digital workbook.

This worksheet is designed to help you to take inventory of all of your debt. Even the $10 that you owe to your cousin! Use the Know What You Owe sheet to list and total all of the debts that you have.

Don't panic if the number scares you! That's why you're reading this book. Over the next few pages, I'll share how you can tackle your debt in manageable phases.

Chapter 3: Stop The Cycle

Despite their very aggressive attempts in college, I managed to not be swayed by the credit card companies offering Visas in exchange for a slice of pizza or a t-shirt. That was one thing that I listened to my dad about . . . at least until I was on my own.

In 2011, I moved mid-way across the country to take my first "real" job in Houston, Texas. By now, you'd think that I was ready to be an adult, but I wasn't. I took a position on a corporate rotational program that allowed me to change roles every six months for two years and be, essentially, coddled the entire time. At least by then, I figured, I'd know what I wanted to do with my life and have my finances somewhat together.

While in Houston, the company hosted a financial education workshop in partnership with a local asset management firm.

I sat in, eager to learn what this financial expert had to say about managing money, because at this point saving $50 was a struggle. Whatever he said was just enough to make me schedule an appointment to discuss hiring him as my financial advisor.

It was the right thing to do after all, right? I obviously didn't know how to manage money so hiring someone to help me do it was the next best alternative.

. . . or so I thought.

I signed a 1-year contract and spent $600 that I couldn't afford to lose, on a less than subpar service.

At the end of it all, I was still broke, busted, and disgusted. I knew no more about money management than I did when I walked into his office.

Our meetings merely consisted of going over my bank statements and him telling me that I needed to spend less money on hair. Even I knew that! I didn't need to pay $600 to have someone state the obvious. I had more than a spending issue and I was hoping that he had the expertise to help me figure out how to fix my finances.

Needless to say, when the company sent a letter asking if I'd like to renew my services, I did the longest eye roll ever and tossed it in the trash.

Hoping to at least find a silver lining in the experience, I remember him encouraging me to get my credit score up. By then, I'd enlisted personal finance books for help and they all said the same thing. So off I went to get a credit card to boost my 500 something score.

DECLINED!

The first card that I applied for was an American Express card. This was a lofty goal for someone with no credit history. But, hey, I'm all about shooting for the stars, so I did.

I remember having my hopes up that they'd somehow accept me and all of my lack of credit. But apparently being an American isn't enough to qualify you for their card.

On to the next one.

A bit discouraged, I decided to go for a less flashy card—basically one with lower standards and perks. I weighed my options from the many commercials that I had seen and applied.

I was approved!

I decided that I'd only use it for items like gas and groceries and pay it off each month.

At least the second part of my plan held true. No matter what, I was diligent about paying off my credit card each month, even if it meant scraping by on everything else.

That's what we all think, right? Even though we can't stick to a diet to save our lives, we somehow believe that we can stay disciplined with spending "free" money.

Well, the joke was on me.

What started out as being solely for groceries and gas, became a vehicle for me to start financing things that I couldn't afford. Things like a vacation to Florida, or even worse, hair extensions! Regardless of the fact that my credit score was indeed rising, my grasp on money was faltering more than ever.

Eventually I came to my senses and realized that I wanted to be out of debt more than I cared about a credit score. And the truth is, you can't have both. You see, in order to have a high credit score, you must always be in debt. So, if I ever wanted to be debt free, I had to dismiss the notion of also having a high credit score.

So, I made my decision.

I cut up the card and closed the account.

The Credit & Debt Cycle

I have a confession to make that may change your mind about getting on this journey of becoming debt free.

Good credit and being debt free very rarely coexist. So, if you're committed to being debt free, be prepared for a significant drop in your credit score.

Here's why . . .

Your credit score is a function of your debt. In a gist, a credit score is a universal way of determining someone's ability to "manage" debt. It takes into account the type of debt that you have, how long you've had it, how many times you've tried to get financing, how much you utilize your debt, and how well you do with making your payments on time. Therefore, without debt, you have no credit.

Now you should understand why it's called "building" your credit. You have to constantly add debt over time in order for your score to improve.

I had to ask myself if I always wanted to be in debt. Furthermore, I had to reason why I even cared about my credit score if I had no intentions of ever borrowing money again.

Here's another confession: *I have no idea what my credit score is.*

You read correctly. I'm writing a personal finance book with no idea what my credit score is.

Before I became debt free, my credit score was one of those things that I harbored over. I had the Credit Karma app on my phone, getting the notifications when my score rose or fell. I was into the game because after all that was the whole point of me getting a credit card—to raise my score.

I'm competitive by nature, so I wanted the highest score possible—not realizing that being the best at debt isn't really a mantle that I want to carry. I realized that boasting about a high credit score was just ignorantly saying that I'm good at paying people back.

Well whoop de doo. I guess I deserved a cookie, right?

So, I stopped worrying about it. At last check a few years ago, it was in the upper 700s, though that really means nothing in my world these days. Instead, I only check my report every so often just to make sure no one has attempted to steal my identity.

I'm sure you're wondering how to manage your finances without regard to your credit? Well, in short, just focus on being able to pay for everything cash. That includes a car and home, if possible.

But, before I jump into those big items, let's focus on how you can manage your day-to-day finances without using debt.

Three Ways To Manage Your Finances Without Debt

I'll admit that quitting debt cold turkey can be a bit of a shocker to your budget. Where you've relied on debt to cover expenses will now have to be covered by cash. So here's how you can prepare for the change:

1. **Implement zero-based budgeting**
   We'll get into the nitty gritty of budgeting in a later section, but it's worth noting here. Allocating every cent that you earn with the help of a budget will make transitioning from credit significantly easier.

   A zero-based budget is essentially creating a budget where zero dollars are left over at the end of the budgeting period. This doesn't mean that you spend all of your money, but it does mean that every penny of your income has an assignment for that pay period. That assignment could be paying a bill, saving, or going toward debt repayment.

Budgeting, in general, is simply you assigning a responsibility to your income before you even receive it. You'll find that when you budget you'll be able to see where adjustments can be made to free up cash for your emergency fund or debt.

2. **Save for emergencies**
   Having an emergency fund is a necessity for living debt free. You will no longer rely on credit cards to bear the brunt of car repairs, medical emergencies, or the like. Instead, you'll need to save a minimum of $1,000 to cover true emergencies that happen.

   True emergencies are those things that are unexpected and need to be addressed immediately. An example would be if your car tire blew and you needed to replace it in order to have transportation. That's something that will require you to spend a significant amount of money that you weren't expecting at the time. Whereas, buying tickets to a Beyoncé concert before they sell out is not an emergency.

   The fact of the matter is the majority of households don't have funds to hedge against emergencies or sudden lapses in income. When you're living paycheck to paycheck, it may seem impossible to put money away for a rainy day, but that's where budgeting comes into play. If you implement a zero-base budget, you'll be able to see where you can free up cash to build your emergency account.

   After you've paid off debt, you'll build your account from $1,000 to six to twelve months' worth of expenses. So, if you suddenly lose your job (which happened to me), you'll have enough in savings to cover the cost of living until you find another stream of income without getting into debt!

3. **Carry cash**

   You may have grown accustomed to swiping at will with your credit card; however, when living a debt free life of discipline, carrying cash is key.

   Once you've allocated how much you'll spend in each area of your zero-based budget, you'll simply withdraw the cash needed to pay for it. You can use cash for groceries, gas, dining out—basically anything that doesn't have to be paid online. Cash automatically creates a limit that you can't go past. No cash, no go!

   One way to do this is to use envelopes, or the cash envelope system. It's just a fancy way of separating your money based on what you've budgeted for. For instance, if your grocery budget it $100, you'll put $100 cash in an envelope labeled "Groceries." Once the envelope is empty, that means you've spent all that's allocated for that line item. It's a matter of fact way to not spend more than you've allocated.

✎ *Action:* It's time for you to cut the cards. If you still owe a balance, then you won't be able to close the account just yet, but what you can do is prevent any payments from being made from it.

Remove your credit card on file from all subscription services and/or bills.

1. Clear all of your web browser history and cache on your computer and phone to get rid of your credit card number and pin so that you can't use them again. *(Do a quick Google search on how to do this.)*
2. DO NOT request another card after the deed has been done.

This is a boss move. You've now removed all safety nets and will need to make sure you actually have cash to pay for everything.

If you've been using your credit cards to pay for your lifestyle it's time to cut some things out.

Chapter 4: Call Your Lender

I remember my conversation with my undergraduate student loan lender like it was yesterday.

"I'd like to separate out my loan groups," I told the woman on the other end of the phone. I had several smaller loans with them that had been combined into groups with one payment.

Though it was intended to make payments more convenient, I knew that if I could get them separated into the smaller loans that they were, I'd be able to pay something off much sooner.

"I don't think you can do that," she said.

Not taking "no" for an answer, I asked her to check with her manager. I learned a long time ago that managers tend to know more than the first person that you talk to.

She came back on the line a few minutes later, "We can have those separated for you. You'll be able to make payments toward them individually."

Success!!

A quick call to my lender allowed me to break my loans up into smaller, more manageable debts. Beyond that though, that call showed that I had an interest in taking care of my responsibility and that I was willing to work *with* them to get it done.

End The Cycle

You may or may not have grown up in a family where avoiding your lender at all costs was normal. Where you were taught that the "bill collector" was the enemy and needed to be treated as an adversary.

When they call, your conditioned response is to dodge. Children are even taught to lie for their parents to avoid them. As a result, it becomes a perpetual and generational cycle of financial recklessness.

To this day, I still have bill collectors calling me for my family member's unpaid debts. How they even managed to get my phone number is beyond me, but that's beside the point. Their lack of responsibility and willingness to create a plan with their lender has caused their debt to now become public knowledge with the intent of embarrassment.

All this can be avoided if you just pick up the phone!

But here's the truth. Your lender is just doing their job. You borrowed the money and you agreed to pay it back and they're just making sure that you hold up your end of the bargain.

It certainly doesn't mean that they should harass you, but it does mean that you've become a slave to the lender. Legally, they have a right to get their money and annoy you in the process.

But what if you truly can't pay them back at the moment? What if you're really underwater, trying to make ends meet and you just can't make the payment that they've established?

Call them.

As much as we'd like to believe that they're the bad guys, the person on the other end of the phone is also a human that's working to feed their own family. That means that they possess an emotion called empathy. It gives them the ability to understand what you're going through and the willingness to help you; however, you'll never be granted that grace if you never call.

Just recently, I shared this tip with my audience on Instagram. I had a collector chime in on the comments and say, "Yes! Please call us. We have repayment options."

At the end of the day, your lender would much rather you pay them something than nothing. That means that they'll work with you to pay something.

Now, calling won't mean that they'll forgive your loans, but it opens the door to negotiate and create a plan that you can actually stick to.

Calling To Discuss Repayment Options

When you're ready to give your lender a call there are a few things that you need to do to prepare. It can be scary addressing your lenders, so it's imperative that you go into the discussion confident and comfortable with your plan.

Here's what you should do beforehand:

- ❑ **Have your account security information.** This may seem like a no brainer, but how many times have you been asked the pin to your account and you couldn't recall it? Make sure you know the security details of your account so that the representative knows it's you and can discuss your account.

- ❑ **Have your most recent statement.** Have your most recent statement available so that you can discuss specific details of your account with the representative. You'll need to know the balance that you owe.

- ❑ **Have a clear and concise explanation for your inability to pay under your current plan.** The fact of the matter is that your lender isn't looking for a long, drawn out sob story. They want to know and understand a reasonable explanation for you needing adjustments to your plan. Have you been laid off? Are you unemployed? Did you take a pay cut? Not wanting to pay is not a reasonable explanation.

- ❑ **Have a well thought out plan and realistic options.** You're calling to discuss options that will benefit both you and the lender. Take a moment beforehand to research other options that are available to you and what you can realistically afford to pay back each month. Have a plan for when you'll be able to make the full payments. Be specific and give them confidence in your efforts and ability to pay them back.

- ❑ **Have evidence of your inability to pay.** Lenders get calls every day from people trying to escape their debt. That includes people who are willing to lie about their financial situation to do so. Don't be one of those people. Be able to provide proof of your current financial situation that supports your inability to make the full payment that was prescribed to you. Things like proof of unemployment will be critical to support your case. Advise the representative that you'll be following up with a letter recapping your information and the agreed upon options. Include any necessary supporting information that is requested during the call.

- ❑ **Have a positive attitude.** Debt can certainly bring you down and talking to your lender can be daunting. Go in with a positive perspective and polite attitude. You'd be surprised at how far being nice can get you with a customer service representative. Also remember, they're human too.

During your conversation, remember to stay calm, polite, and focus on the reason that you're calling.

Here are some options that you may have when negotiating with your lender:

- **Defer payments/hardship plan** - If you've lost your job or are unemployed, this may be an option for you. Your lender may make arrangements to either defer your payments to resume at a later date or lower your minimum payment, interest, and fees.

- **Reduce minimum monthly payment** - If you're unable to cover the full amount of your monthly minimum payment, your lender may agree to reducing the payment. Though it may cost you more in the long run, it is a temporary way to relieve the financial strain.

- **Lower interest rate** - Similar to the monthly payment, reducing your interest rate will also reduce that amount that you have to pay each month.

- **Remove past late fees** - If you're struggling to make your monthly minimum payment, then paying additional late fees will make it almost impossible to get current. Waiving this fee will remove the additional burden and financial obligation. The key however, is to not be late again.

- **Lump sum settlement** - This option entails negotiating with your lender to pay less than what you owe. In order for this to be a viable option in your situation, you'd need a significant amount of cash that you can use to pay off your settled amount immediately.

Get It In Writing

If you find that your lender is willing to negotiate with you, make sure that you get the terms of your agreement in writing. When discussing your accounts, make it a habit to get the customer service representative's name and contact information for your record.

At the conclusion of the call, review your agreed upon plan with the representative. Confirm that they have documented this information in their files and request a follow up email and letter outlining your agreement. Take the further step of sending a letter recapping your agreement, along with any necessary documents that are needed to proceed with your new plan.

Get clear details about when the changes will take effect on your account. Make a note on your calendar to follow up on this date to ensure that what was agreed upon has been updated.

Chapter 5: Start Your Debt Snowball

The first payment that I made toward seriously getting out of debt was tough!

I had just gotten my savings account over $1,000 after years of failed attempts of putting aside $50 per month. Now I was going to literally take every cent above that $1,000 and put it toward my smallest debt.

I contemplated not doing it. Afterall, with over $1,000 in savings, I could just stop adding to my savings account and put those funds toward paying down my debt. But, when would I ever have that much money to put toward debt at one time again?

I closed my eyes and did it.

In December 2013, I made my first lump sum payment toward my student loans.

I had never spent so much money at one time before! Yet after putting it toward my debt, not only was I shell shocked, but I was extremely excited to finally be paying off my debt!

Days prior I had read Dave Ramsey's *Total Money Makeover* book, where I learned about a debt payoff method called the "Debt Snowball." I was intrigued by this approach to paying off debt because it was simple. You attack your smallest debt first, pay it off quickly, and build momentum to quickly pay off your other debts.

If paying off debt was that simple, I could get with it.

I later discovered that there are lots of other coined methods out there, but the snowball method is what worked for me, and therefore, is what I teach. Nonetheless, I'll also share information on another method that you can leverage to pay off debt. First, let's explore the snowball method.

The Debt Snowball

In his book, Dave explains his very simple method of paying off your smallest debt first and working your way up to paying off your biggest loan. The idea is that once you pay off the smaller debts you can apply the money that would have gone toward those payments to your next largest debt.

By starting with the smallest loan, you're able to achieve a quick win that will give you the confidence and momentum to continue paying off your other debts quickly—like a snowball rolling down a hill!

Here's how to implement the debt snowball.

Step 1. Save at least $1,000 for emergencies

One thing is certain about life—things come up. And because you'll begin putting all of your extra cash toward paying off your debt, it's imperative that you have something set aside to cover emergencies.

If you're a working, single adult, having at least $1,000 put away in savings should be adequate; however, it may not be enough if you have a family and kids or if you're very risk averse. Either way, put at least $1,000 away in a high yield savings account (I'll talk more about high yield savings accounts in a later chapter) in case of an emergency.

If you're like me, you're probably thinking, "I don't have $1000." Trust me, there are ways that you can save up $1,000 quickly. I share my recommended methods when discussing how to increase your income. But, as a quick tip, if you can find a way to set aside at least $11/day for 3 months, you will save $1,000 without even knowing it.

Step 2. List out your debts from smallest largest

The second step in the debt snowball process is listing out your debts from smallest to largest— regardless of the interest rate.

This is what makes this method different from others. The focus is not on getting rid of the highest interest rate first. Instead, the focus is getting rid of your smallest debt as soon as possible so that you can free up cash to pay off the next one.

When you pay off your smallest debt as soon as possible, it gives you a quick win that will give you the momentum to keep going. It's like losing weight. If you can lose 5 lbs quickly, you'll be more motivated to keep going to lose the next ten or fifteen.

This part is all a mental game. Get wins quickly is the mission.

Step 3. Pay the minimum payment on all of your debt except the smallest

In order to get rid of your smallest debt, you have to start putting extra money toward it. That means you'll need to free up any additional cash that you have. The first way to do this is by paying the minimum due on every other debt.

Paying minimum on the other debt ensures that you don't go into default while you put all of your extra money and attention on paying off your smallest debt. Divided focus will slow down progress, so focus on the one debt at a time.

Step 4. Increase your income

If you're wondering where the extra funds will come from to put toward your smallest debt, this step is your answer. In step four, you'll work to increase your income. This is where picking up a second job, cutting expenses, and getting creative come into play.

I've dedicated a whole chapter to this topic alone, so you don't have to figure it out just yet. Just know that bringing in extra cash really isn't as hard as you think it is. Over the years I've discovered that if we have the right motivation and a desire to get something, we'll find a way to fund it. Getting out of debt is no different. If you're passionate enough about it and want it bad enough, you'll always find a way to make extra money to meet your goal.

Step 5. Put your extra cash toward your smallest debt

Now that you have extra cash, it's time to start putting it toward that smallest debt. As extra cash flows in and you find "extra" money in your budget, begin making additional payments toward your smallest loan. Pile on as much cash as possible to get rid of them quickly.

When making extra payments toward your debt, it's important that you communicate with your lender that you want the payments applied to your principal balance. In most cases, they'll do this anyway, but always ask to be sure. Remember, lenders bank off of interest on your principal balance and they would much rather you apply the least amount to your balance as possible.

Step 6. Pay off your smallest debt and apply that money to your next debt

With all of those extra payments, you'll have your smallest debt paid off in no time. Once it's paid off, apply the money that would have gone toward that debt repayment to the next smallest debt. This is not extra money for you to spend!

Immediately apply it to your next loan and continue the method. You'll still be paying minimum on your other loans while putting as much extra cash as possible toward this loan.

Step 7. Repeat until all of your debt is paid off

Continue steps one through six until you have all of your debt paid off. It's a simple cycle of focusing on one debt at a time and putting all of your resources toward making sure it gets paid off.

The Debt Avalanche Method

The debt avalanche method is a debt repayment method where you pay off debt from the highest interest rate to the lowest. With this exception, you'd still follow the steps outlined in the debt snowball method.

The pro of this method is that it enables you to save money on interest; however, the con is that your largest interest may be for a very large debt. Because paying off a large debt takes time, this can be discouraging and cause you to lose momentum.

Both methods rely on the underlying principle of putting as much extra money toward your debt as possible to expedite your payoff. Regardless of which method you leverage, the point is to just start and stick to it!

Creating Your Debt Payoff Plan

Tracking your debt repayment and seeing your progress makes a significant impact on quickly paying off your loans. Again, if you can see the 5 lbs off of the scale, you'll be more motivated to continue the process.

While doing the debt snowball, I created an excel sheet to track my payments and to calculate when my loans would be paid off. Though, while writing this book, I found a tool that is ridiculously helpful in creating your debt payoff plan for you, based on the snowball or avalanche method. It takes all of your debt information and creates what I'd consider a debt amortization chart.

That tool is Undebt.it and it can be accessed at *bit.ly/Undebtit*, where you can sign up for a free account.

It's a platform that helps you manage paying off your debt by providing a free online debt snowball calculator, progress reports, and payoff plan options. Undebt.it creates a debt payoff chart that shows you exactly how much you should allocate toward each debt every month and when the debt will be paid off.

In addition to giving you an easy to understand and easy to use debt payoff schedule, Undebt.it also provides a comparison of the total amount paid, interest, and debt repayment time using the debt snowball or avalanche method versus just paying the minimum amounts.

I find this tool perfect for monitoring your debt payoff and having visuals to show where you're at in your process. It's definitely what I wish existed when I was paying off my debt.

If you're not into the digital space, I've also provided a debt payoff tracker that you can print and write on in the Everyday Chick's Guide to Money digital workbook.

Chapter 6: Increase Your Income

The key to paying off your debt quickly using the debt snowball method is to increase your income.

This may sound like another "easier said than done" remedy, but it really can be easier than you think.

You see, increasing your income doesn't automatically mean that you need to get another job. Although that is one way, it isn't the only.

In this chapter, I'm going to explore ways that you can quickly increase your income without getting another job. I'll tackle things like side hustles and salary increases in the next chapter.

Lower Your Expenses

If your aim is to pay off your debt as quick as possible, then you'll need every penny available to you to do so. Even the one that you find in your couch.

The simplest way to find extra money is where money already is. That means your expenses and the things that you spend money on every month.

Typically, there are a few items that we fund that we can afford to axe from our monthly expenses list. Just look through your latest bank statements to determine what is a necessity and what isn't.

Because cutting things can be hard, let me give you a clear understanding of what a necessity is versus what isn't.

NECESSITIES

Your necessities are the things that you absolutely need to survive—and I'm not talking your cell phone. It's the bare minimum of human existence and without it, you arguably can't survive.

Food

Food is obviously a necessity that we need to sustain life; however, it does not mean that it has to be take out, dine in, or fast food for every meal. Properly planning and preparing your meals can not only save you money, but it can also improve your health.

On average, I would pay about $7 per day to eat at the cafeteria at work. Though convenient, it totaled around $1,800 per year and lots of pounds on the scale. To put that money toward debt, I started meal planning, buying groceries, and prepping my meals to take to lunch.

Try limiting the number of times that you eat out by replacing it with meals prepared at home. This will help lower your expenses when it comes to food.

Shelter

Shelter is also a necessity of life, but much like food, you don't have to have the creme de la creme to survive. Consider downsizing your living space to reduce your cost for shelter.

When I began my debt free journey, I was living in a three-bedroom townhouse that cost a lot to heat and cool. So instead of continuing to pay a significant amount of money for space that I didn't need, I downsized into a less expensive apartment. Doing so allowed me to free up cash to put toward my debt.

Downsizing can seem like a scary thing to do; however, if you're dedicated to getting out of debt, you'll take the necessary steps to save on such a major expense as living costs.

Consider moving into a smaller and less expensive space temporarily to free up the cash to pay off your debt sooner.

Clothing

Clothing is another necessity of life that requires money. Like the aforementioned, you don't need the most expensive items to survive.

Instead of going on a massive shopping spree or spending tons of money on clothes, consider purchasing items that are on sale or thrift. If you must purchase new clothes for whatever reason, purchase for quality, not quantity. Invest in pieces that will last you a long time so that you don't have to buy clothes frequently.

Transportation

Unless you live within walking distance of work, the grocery store, and other primary locations, transportation is a need. The mode, however, is debatable.

In your journey to become debt free, your primary objective when it comes to transportation should be getting from point A to point B.

If you're a city dweller, you likely have the advantage of public transportation that isn't much of a financial burden, so you probably don't need a car to survive. In that case, you could sell it to free up cash to put toward debt.

However, if you live in a rural area where this isn't the case, you likely own a car.

In this case, the question becomes, "How much car do you need?"

Did you know that the average car payment in the US is upwards of $500 per month? That doesn't include fuel or maintenance that's necessary for it to be drivable. Add on taxes and registration fees and you've got yourself a mammoth of a bill each month.

What debt could you pay off with an extra $500 per month?

I get it, your car payment may not be $500 per month, but the reality is that most people still own a car that is well above their financial means. Of course, they'll never admit it. Who wants to broadcast the fact that their Beamer is the reason that they can't seem to pay off their student loans from 15 years ago.

The make and model of a car is a status symbol to most people. And for this reason, most people won't set aside their pride to trade in their shiny, depreciating automobile for a ride that's just designed to get them from point A to point B.

The question all boils down to, "How much are you willing to sacrifice?"

That's the question that I always asked my personal finance coaching clients.

How badly do you want to get out of debt?

If you want it badly enough, you'll learn to put aside the pride and get rid of all the unnecessary niceties in life in exchange for things that will get the job done in the interim.

There's one story that seems to stick with me every time I graze this topic.

It's a story that I heard during a debt free call on Dave Ramsey's radio show. During his show, Dave allows guests to come on to do their debt free scream. They share their story of getting out of debt and then, at the conclusion, scream "We're debt free!"

This particular day, a couple called in for their scream. As Dave asked his usual questions about what the debt was and how they amassed it, they began to share their story of purchasing two brand new Beamers as their status symbols for "making it."

They had graduated college, landed decent paying jobs, but they were still broke. Yet, they still managed to believe that they could afford not one, but two, brand spanking new BMWs.

Well, as you might imagine, it backfired—like it always does. They were covered in debt and needed a way out.

Do you know what they did? They didn't hang on to their status symbols. They didn't continue to ride around in the very thing that was keeping them bound in debt.

Nope. Instead, they did what most people wouldn't. They sold their nice, shiny Beamers and got hoopties instead.

Talk about an ego blow!

I'm sure they thought about all of the things that their friends and family would say.

"Are they going through a hard time?" "Did he lose his job?"

But amidst the whispers that I'm sure floated about, they took a big gulp and did it. The result? Well, they're debt free.

How bad do you want it? Can you handle a temporary sacrifice for a greater reward?

The Other Stuff

Now that we've covered your necessities, let's take a peek at the things that tend to creep up in our budget, but aren't necessary to live.

It's what I like to call "nice"ssities. They're nice to have, but not necessary to survive. Some common expenses that fall under this category are:

- Cable
- Eating out
- Nail and hair appointments
- Gym memberships
- Subscription services

I'm sure you're probably screaming, "STOP THE PRESSES!! I know she's not talking about my nails!"

Indeed I am.

Back when I was broke and in debt, I miraculously found ways to pay for my nails to be perfectly manicured every two weeks.

Now, I'll admit that I was able to save significantly because I didn't get acrylics; however, I was still spending a minimum of $80 per month.

At that time, $80 was two minimum payments on my largest student loan debt. Instead of realizing that, I kept spending money on something that temporarily made me feel cute.

Eventually, I figured things out and stopped shelling out money. Instead of going to the nail salon, I opted to buy some nail polish and paint my own nails. I've since just kept it even simpler and don't wear polish at all—a time and cost savings.

As a woman, I get that we want to look our best and be presentable, but I'd argue that this is possible for free, or at least next to nothing! Although you'd like to think that you can't paint your own nails or do your own hair, you can—or at least find less expensive alternatives that will free up cash to pay off debt.

I'm admittedly a proud student of both YouTube and Google Universities. I'm constantly on a quest to learn how to do things myself so that I can save money, where it makes sense.

Sell things

Making quick cash is a part of the debt payoff game. The quicker you can make cash to put toward your debt, the quicker they can get paid off.

If you took my advice earlier about downsizing your living, then it's also a great time for you to sell things that can't go with you to your new, smaller space.

To help bring in some additional cash outside of my 9 to 5, I decided to sell unused or gently worn clothes and handbags. I no longer had a need for them and they were just taking up space.

Selling items that you no longer need doesn't have to be as hard as you think. The Internet and social media have made getting rid of junk so easy that there's really no excuse not to sell things online.

Here are a few ways to sell:

Host a yard sale

Nothing is easier to help get some quick cash than to host a good ole fashioned yard sale. There are people whose weekend activities include finding yard/estate sales to thrift for items. They're the people you're looking for.

Set up a quick table in your yard, or if you're in an apartment, ask to set up shop in your common area.

Label and neatly organize the items that you're selling to make shopping a breeze for your customers.

Since we're going old fashion, you can promote your yard sale with a handmade sign and maybe some enticing words like, "One of a kind pieces!" People love having unique, exclusive items that can't be found anywhere else.

Remember, the intent is to make quick cash on things that you no longer want or need. So if someone pulls out their negotiating skills and gives you an offer lower than your ticketed price, don't be too prideful to not accept.

Most yard sales are cash deals, so make sure that you have change available for big bills. You can also get a little snazzy by getting a Square or PayPal debit card reader that you can connect directly to your smartphone! Just keep in mind that these payment processing services will take their cut, so you may want to up your price to cover the additional costs.

Sell on sites like eBay or Poshmark

eBay has long been a place for people to sell custom items or things that they no longer want or use. Today, there are lots of other sites that have popped up, including Poshmark.

These sites serve as easy platforms that allow you to transact sales online with customers. Each has their own rules that you must abide by, but the general concept is the same:

1. Create an account
2. Link your payment information (ex. PayPal)
3. Post your items
4. Get a sale

5. Pay the host site their cut
6. Get money deposited to your account

The downside of selling online is that you have to pay and arrange for shipping. Afterall, you can't just take someone's money and not ship their goods.

Most pros know to include shipping in the cost of the item. You can get an estimate from your local UPS or shipping store. Again, the goal here is to get as much margin as possible—accounting for shipping and hosting fees.

Take your clothes to a local consignment shop

Selling clothes to a consignment shop is another option to get quick cash.

If you don't want to give your clothes away to charity or to an individual in need, you can always sell them to a consignment shop. These shops will pay cash for your clothes, only to resell them at a higher price.

Personally, I haven't found much success here, as they tend to give you pennies for your nicely kept items; however, it's worth a try! Depending on your city and the brand of your clothes, you may get a good deal.

Create your own consignment shop on Facebook or Instagram

How about forgetting the middleman and just selling on your own? Sounds like a good idea to me!

I actually sold my clothing items on Instagram and Facebook. It was as simple as posting a picture of the item, listing the price in the description, and telling those who were interested in buying it to comment or message their email address so that I can send them a PayPal invoice.

Ultimately, the sale went to the first person to provide their information and paid. I later packaged the item and shipped it with a tracking number.

Now Facebook has a marketplace where people in the same area can sell their items to each other.

Much like selling on sites like eBay, you'll still need to make arrangements for shipping, pickup, or delivery. So don't forget to include that in your pricing.

These are all quick ways to make some extra cash. But, let's talk about a long-term strategy for consistently making more money.

Let's explore how to Build your Bank!

Section 3: Build Your Bank

Chapter 7: Make More Money

If you want to build bank, there's one thing that you need to understand: the money cycle.

The money cycle is a term that I coined a few years ago in an effort to simplify the three basics steps that you must take with your money in order for you to build wealth.

In order for you to master finances, you have to abide by the three basics principles of money. These principles are age old and reliable and are what the wealthy understand and use to continue to build wealth. It's what you're going to apply to maximize your money to build your bank.

The three basic principles that you need to understand about money in order to build wealth are:

1. Money must be made
2. Money must be managed
3. Money must be multiplied

Together, in that specific order, these three factors make up the money cycle. You must first make money, then manage it, and multiply it in a continuous cycle if you want to build wealth.

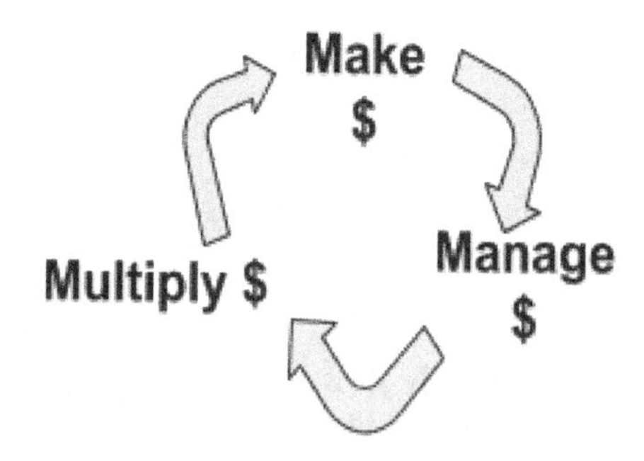

If these principles are applied correctly and sequentially, you'll be on an inevitable road to building wealth that will span generations.

Let's dig a bit further into these principles and how you can apply them to your finances.

You Must Make Money

The first principle that makes up the money cycle is that you must make money.

Simple enough, right?

We're taught this very basic principle from a young age. If you were fortunate enough to earn an allowance, you knew that it was only in exchange for completing chores around the house or doing well in school.

Your parents or guardian taught you very early on that money is earned, not merely given. Unbeknownst to you, a very important concept was being ingrained in you—how an economy works.

The basis of any economy, or financial system, is generating money. For a true economy to exist, there has to be an exchange of goods or services for some monetary compensation. In fact, it's important to note that money is only made by two means.

Money is made (not acquired) by two means and two means only:

1. You provide a service in exchange for it
2. You provide a product in exchange for it

The old adage is correct in saying that money doesn't grow on trees. You must provide something in exchange for it, and those who master the art of exchanging more valuable products or services become those who make the most money.

Since we're talking about building bank, it's important to state that the goal is not just to make money. The goal is to make *lots* of money.

I imagine that the saints who have been taught that to be poor is to be holy are probably cringing after reading that statement. Well, cringe on . . . and keep reading.

Allow me to step on my soapbox . . .

I am fully persuaded that God created us to prosper in spirit, health, and wealth. Though we should not *love* money, we can acquire lots of it in order to create a legacy for our families and to advance God's work on earth.

Ministry cannot happen without money. Those wells that need to be built in impoverished nations can't happen without money. The child that needs a scholarship for school can't go without money. Even the church that you may worship in can't operate without money.

So, if all of this is to be the responsibility of believers, don't you think that we ought to have money?

The fact is that money is a necessity of life and those with lots of it can make a huge difference in the world—whether good or bad. I want you to be one of those difference makers who does good things with the money that you earn.

Now, I'll pretend like I received a resounding, "Amen, sister!" and step down from my soapbox.

Becoming More Valuable

The more valuable the service or product that you provide, the more money you're able to make in exchange for it. Additionally, the scarcer the product or service that you provide, the more money you'll be able to demand for it.

It's the good old concepts of value and supply and demand.

So, what exactly is value?
Well, in general, value is the worth—usually expressed in money—that you assign to something. Items that are termed as "priceless" are things that all the money in the world couldn't afford.

Your children, for example, are priceless. I assume that they're worth so much to you that no amount of money would make you part with them.

But what about your skills? Say, your ability to speak to an audience, teach a lesson, or even prepare a meal. How much are those things worth?

Well, I hope that you believe in your own skills enough to assign a high value to them; however, in many cases, the world has come to a consensus on what many skills are worth to the economy. This is done in the form of average career salaries, average costs of services, or suggested retail prices on products.

The monetary value assigned to either a service or product is an indicator of how much something is valued in the economy. For instance, professional athletes get paid millions more than teachers. What does that say? Well, sports and entertainment are valued more than education—and believe me, it shows.

The value assigned to these things is based on four factors:

1. Availability
2. Experience/Expertise
3. Delivery
4. Impact

Let's talk availability.

Availability

Do you remember playing the game The Oregon Trail growing up? I'm talking about way back when there was no such thing as Wi-Fi and you couldn't get on the internet without tying up the phone line.

Well, if you don't recall, this game was designed to educate players on the life of families migrating west on the Oregon trail during the 19th-century. But like most games, there was a fun aspect. My favorite was panning for gold. If your player found gold, they ultimately found wealth. Why? Because gold was hard to mine, and therefore, was scarce.

When something is scarce—say a limited edition —it automatically makes that product or service extremely high in value.

Want to know why Lebron James gets to sign nearly $100 million-dollar contracts? His ability to handle the basketball is one of a kind. Arguably, no one in this generation has the skill set and ball handle of Lebron. As a result, they pay him extremely large sums of money to display his talent.

So, what does that mean for you and increasing your value to earn more money? It means that if you want to be able to exchange a skill or product that you have for more money, it needs to be scarce, or within a specific niche.

Experience & Expertise

Experience and expertise are the next two components of valuation. The more knowledge and experience that you have around a subject matter, the more valuable you become in the economy. Being a subject matter expert in a relevant area is a guaranteed way to always make money.

Let me clearly state the experience goes hand in hand with expertise. It's cited that in order to become an expert as something, you must do it for a least 10,000 hours. So those makeup "gurus" on YouTube who just learned what foundation is yesterday aren't exactly experts.

The more time that you are able to dedicate to a skill, the more you learn and can exchange that knowledge for money.

Delivery

Have you ever gotten a gift and before you could even open it, you were wowed by the packaging? Before you even knew what was inside, you had already given kudos to the person who gave it to you. You did this because delivery matters.

It's the reason why you wrap gifts at Christmas or literally kill the environment by stuffing a bag with useless tissue paper. You want to deliver your gift with your best foot forward.

A part of valuation is delivery. Your delivery is how you package and present your expertise to consumers in your niche. If you deliver it well, then you're able to charge more for what you're providing, but poor delivery means poor pockets.

A few years ago, I began following a well-known entrepreneur and speaker on social media. On one of the days that I decided to visit her website, I stumbled across her page for speaking requests and coaching. I sat stunned when I saw the amount of money that she demanded for her services.

At minimum, she charged $25,000 to speak at an event. I read on . . .

She went on to justify her costs by stating the number of years that she has been speaking professionally (her expertise), the specific areas that she's an expert in (her scarcity/niche), and her ability to move the audience to change as shown by reviews (delivery and impact).

She knew the four pillars of valuation, and as a result, was able to command and get (the important part) what she asked for.

But of course, having a niche, expertise, and delivery means nothing if there is no impact.

Impact

How many times have you sat in a church service listening to a preacher eloquently deliver his well prepared and researched sermon, only for it to have no impact on your life? If you're petty, you probably didn't put anything in the offering plate, did you?

Maybe church isn't your thing. Instead, you may have invested in a service that was packaged well—nice website, nice branding—only to find out that you wasted your money because it had no impact or didn't do what was promised.

Whatever the case, we've all experienced something that was packaged well, but had absolutely no impact on our lives. It probably left you unsatisfied and even disappointed.

That is because the four factors of valuation must be present in order for a product or service(s) to be worthwhile and allow for you to demand money for it. Your product or service must impact your consumer in a positive way.

So, if you want to make more money, here is a general rule of thumb:

Provide value by solving someone's very specific problem. The harder the problem—requiring more expertise, experience—the more impact and, ultimately, the more more you'll make.

One of the highest paid careers is that of a surgeon. That's because the skill necessary to perform the service and impact of it are extremely high.

Contrarily, a teenager getting paid to work at a car wash over the summer gets paid next to nothing because their job doesn't require any unique or niche skills. It doesn't take much experience or expertise. Not much effort needs to be put into the delivery, and it is very low impact.

Get Paid For Your Value

Once you've applied the principles of increasing your value in the market, you can now demand compensation for it.

It's important to remember that even in the workplace, you're not just an employee. Now that you've learned what the principles of making money are—that is exchanging a product or service for it—you should now consider yourself a service provider to your employer. So, let's talk about your service fee.

Unfortunately, as women we are grossly underpaid compared to our male counterparts. The narrative is even worse for women of color.

Studies show that on average women make less than half of what men who do the same job make. That's obviously a problem!

To help close this gender wage gap, we're charged to advocate on our own behalf to make sure we get paid according to our value and not according to our gender.

That means negotiations.

Negotiating can be a scary word. We've seen the movies where men are dressed in suits playing hardball across an expensive conference room table. It doesn't seem appealing by any means, but it is necessary.

I'll admit that I'm not an expert negotiator, despite taking trainings on it. In fact, when it came to negotiating the purchase price of our home, I wanted to concede and chicken out. It wasn't until my husband stepped in that I had the courage to continue negotiating with the realtor and ultimately arrive at a price that we could agree on.

Nonetheless, I've found resources that continue to help me build my negotiating skills and confidence. One such resource is my friend and career coach, Danielle Ayodele.

I featured Danielle on my podcast for an episode specifically on negotiating your salary. In fact, I used myself as the subject since I was going through my own salary negotiation at the time. She did an amazing job of live coaching me on the show, and as a result of her support, I was able to get the title and salary that I wanted uncontested! With her help, I received a 15% increase in my salary.

Here's what I learned from that situation:

1. *If you don't ask, it won't be given.* I am sure my employer would have been content with me doing more work for the same pay, but I wasn't. I built up the courage to initiate the conversation and ultimately command more pay.

2. *You have to know your value, and so does your employer.* What made this process easy was my ability to show my value in the workplace. I was known as a problem solver and was able to share a litany of ways that I had positively impacted the organization. Therefore, I could justify asking for more money.

3. *There's always room in the budget.* Companies will always find ways to compensate a valuable employee. I've been on the other side of the hiring table and watched as there was miraculously $5,000 more in the budget to hire a stellar candidate. Be great and know that the budget has room.

Though this has been my most significant pay increase throughout my years of working, I've been able to acquire bonuses and salary increases throughout my career. There are a few tips that I'd like to offer to the career women reading this book who'd like to start getting paid what they are worth.

First, performance should be your foremost priority. I'd guess that you're probably already one of those women. Nonetheless, you need to make your value known throughout the organization.

One thing that I started leveraging early in my career was feedback from my managers. I solicited constant feedback to ensure that I was performing to expectations. I knew what to do that would garner the highest ratings and, therefore, the highest pay.

Second, network. Throughout my early career, I used every available opportunity to network with influential people within my organization. These people may not have set my salary, but they had the ear of the people who did. I made sure that I was also an asset to them by helping them solve a problem within their job.

Take it upon yourself to solve a problem for someone outside of your department or in leadership. Everyone in the organization should know who you are even if you don't work directly with or for them. One of my biggest and unexpected bonuses during my early career came from an executive that I never met, but solved a tremendous problem for.

Today, the CEO of the organization that I work for has dubbed me the Chief Problem Solver. Be the problem solver in your organization and make sure you get compensated for it.

I'd recommend checking out the book *The Secrets of Six Figure Women* by Barbara Stanny. This book gets behind the psychology of high earning women and the things that you must do to reach that financial mark. It's a great companion to this book if you're truly ready to start building wealth.

Increasing Your Sources Of Income

Traditionally, we've been taught that in order to make any decent amount of money, we needed to get an education, find a job at a stable company, then climb the corporate ladder.

That's definitely the bare bones way of making money that provided sufficient income for our grandparents. Now, not so much.

I've already mentioned that money can only be made in exchange for a product or service. So in theory, when you're working your 9 to 5 job, you're exchanging your services for a paycheck.

With that in mind, all of the concepts of valuation apply on your job. If you have a specific skill set that is scarce within the company, along with some expertise and experience, packaged and delivered in a great attitude, promptness, and it will impact to the bottom line, you've got the makings of being well paid.

But the problem is, at some point you'll reach a limit. Either a limit in the time that you have to provide those services or a limit on the amount of money that the company can afford to pay you.

What do you do then?

Well, you learn how to leverage those same skills to make money outside of your traditional job. You create another source of income.

The ultimate goal that you should have when it comes to making money is to no longer exchange time for money. True financial freedom is also freedom of time. It's when you're able to stop trading hours for dollars.

We want to allow our products and services to be available apart from us. This is what's called passive income. It is income that is generated without you having to be actively involved in acquiring it.

Passive Income Ideas

Nothing is more pleasant than waking up to an email letting me know that I've just made money from a passive income source that I've set up months or even years ago. That is the true definition of easy money.

These income sources don't start making money overnight. They require time and effort upfront, but will serve as a stream of income in the future. Let's explore some ways that you can increase your sources, or streams, of income.

Write a book

Before publishing my first book, *They That Wait: A Guide to Living a Life that Honors God* in 2015, I had no idea that it would still continue to generate revenue for me years later. To be quite honest, I didn't know what I expected of the book other than it being the pinnacle of my blogging career at that point.

Today, that same book—which still bears my maiden name—continues to generate sales on Amazon, Kindle, and when I speak at events.

Though I invested a lot of time writing and editing my book those years ago, it's a product that allows me to still bring in income, literally in my sleep.

Here's the truth. I never imagined being an author, let alone twice. I'm sure you may not have either; however, I know that everyone has a story to tell that can ultimately help someone while also providing another source of income.

Here's the thing: *It's not as hard you think.*

You don't have to write a novel, have a literary agent, or even have any upfront money. All you need is an idea, a bit of time, and a computer or tablet with access to the Internet.

Sites like Amazon Kindle Direct Publishing allow you to publish your own books free of charge and they'll even take care of printing and shipping. If you don't have the funds to pay someone to format your book for publishing or to design your cover, no worries! Their tool allows you to download pre-formatted book templates and to create your own book cover design.

You can immediately publish your new book to Amazon or purchase copies to sell on your own.

Sell digital products

The Internet is the ultimate source for information. Each second, people are scouring the web to find a solution to a problem that they're having or to find the answer to a burning question. Why not be one of those answers to their problems or questions?

The term "infopreneur" was coined for people who do just that. They are the pioneers who provide resources of information to an ever seeking world. There are a few ways that you can take advantage of this new phenomenon.

Sell e-books

If writing a lengthier book isn't up your alley, you can take a shot at creating an e-book. Today, e-books are the new books on the market. You can easily create an e-book to sell as a PDF file without even having a website!

E-books lower the barrier of entry because they don't have to be long and you can create as many as you'd like. In fact, Cici of @TheSixFigureChick on Instagram has built a 7-figure empire solely from selling e-books and other digital products.

If you're not interested in writing a book, but think you have the skills to woo audiences with your words, try becoming a freelance writer. Though this can be leveraged as a side hustle and not really passive income, I think that it's worth mentioning here.

There are tons of people who don't have the skills or time to write content and would be willing to pay you to do it on their behalf. Sites like Upwork and Fivver allow you to create a profile to advertise your services, secure clients, and get paid.

Holly Johnson, a fellow personal finance blogger, was able was able to create a six-figure freelance writing career. She now teaches others how to do the same. You can access her course through the Everyday Chick's Guide to Money digital workbook.

Create an online course

This concept of providing online courses for specific topics has taken the Internet by storm. In fact, entrepreneur Danielle Leslie reached over $1M in sales in 2018 just by showing people how to create online courses.

I was able to witness the power of creating courses as a passive income source with a client of mine. Within the first week of her course launching, she generated multi 4-figures in sales.

Platforms like Thinkific, Teachable, and Kajabi offer easy to use tools for creating and hosting your online course. They even provide free training on how to get started in this booming niche. Courses range from kids yoga to starting a blog. If you have something that people want to learn, create a course!

Early on in my business, I created two small courses that were able to generate a few hundred dollars in a few days. It is definitely something that I'll leverage again to generate passive income.

Drop ship products

Ever thought about starting your own t-shirt line? Or, have you wondered how so many people are suddenly selling t-shirts without even having a printing shop?

Well, the answer to that question is drop shipping.

Drop shipping is the concept of having an external company manage the production and shipment of items that you sell. Though they'll get a piece of the pie, you'll still be able to walk away with the majority of the profits.

Drop shipping is also the wonder that has a lot of your cousins and old classmates selling hair extensions. Yep! I just outed them! Now you know the secret to the booming hair business!

Companies manage the acquisition of the hair, packaging, and shipping of the extensions to customers. Some will even create your website for you!

I've seen quotes from $399 to $3,000 upfront cost for this service; however, if done correctly, you could make that up within a few sales.

In the case of t-shirts, you can literally start for free. I've personally created my own t-shirt designs on a free site called Canva and had them printed and shipped through a company called Printful. That means that anyone can come on my site and order a t-shirt and I don't have to worry about a thing except getting paid.

Companies like these also have the capability to print books, other clothing items, mugs, and paper goods. So, if you have a creative idea for products, consider drop shipping as a viable source of passive income.

Become a brand affiliate

It's not uncommon to see an Instagram post or YouTube video with #ad or #sponsored beneath it. That's because we've entered the era of influencer marketing.

Influencer marketing is a very new concept brought on by the height of social media. Brands and companies are leveraging people with a large audience to place products and get much better returns than a traditional advertising campaign.

Think about it. If you saw your favorite YouTuber or person that you follow on Instagram wearing some really dope shoes, you'd likely want to buy them—even if they're being paid to wear them. Think "athlete endorsements," but on a much smaller scale.

But the truth of the matter is that you don't have to have a huge audience to start making money from brands. As an affiliate, you can also get a kick back from promoting some of your favorite products that you use.

My favorite brand affiliate programs is Amazon Affiliates.

As a blogger, I am able to share affiliate links to items that I use with my readers. When they use the link, I am able to make a commission and they aren't charged anything extra. I merely get compensated for recommending the product or service to them.

The cool thing about affiliate links is that you don't have to have a website to use them. You can just as easily use your social media pages to share your links with others; however, with the growing popularity around it, laws have been created to protect consumers. When sharing affiliate links, you have to disclose that information so that people can make the choice to use it or not.

Start A Side Hustle

Though the name of the game is passive income, it'd be unrealistic to believe that the examples provided will allow you to replace your 9 to 5 income immediately. Like all things that yield a return, it takes time to build up.

While you're building up your passive income sources, it doesn't hurt to have extra "active" income sources outside of your regular job.

Side hustles are activities that make you money outside of your 9 to 5. It's your hustle on the side.

Over the years, I've come to know doctors, lawyers, and even veterinarians who have side hustles. Yes, even people making well over six-figures found the need to have additional streams of income and so should you!

There's no rocket science to starting a side hustle. It's as simple as finding something that you're good at and monetizing it.

Think about the young girl in your neighborhood who does hair out of her home or your neighbor who sells her famous pies. These people are leveraging their gifts and talents to bring in extra cash.

I'll admit that the thought of doing work outside of your 9 to 5 can seem overwhelming, but I assure you that it's well worth it for reaching your financial goals.

It wasn't too long ago that I was on the fence about starting my side hustle. Even though I had been blogging for years and making some passive income, I knew that I could do more with my skills outside of my corporate career.

My gift is the ability to recognize inefficiencies in processes and improve them. It's literally what I do on a day-to-day basis and could probably do with my eyes closed. Some would call it my zone of genius.

Not only am I good at improving processes, but I also have a knack for technology.

I designed my first website in college and have continued to master online systems since. People are often surprised when the answer to, *"Who did your website?"* is me.

Although I had these skills that I knew were needed by others, I hesitated for years. It wasn't until late 2018 that I finally decided to offer my skills to the open market as a consultant.

I didn't wait for anyone's permission or seek to get any validation through a certification. Instead, what I found was that the services I offered didn't exist in the market. Every client that I encountered said the same thing, "I don't know anyone else who's doing what you're doing, but I need it!"

I couldn't Google what I was doing or find a mentor. Instead, I just did what was in my heart to do.

After booking my first client in late 2018, my side hustle grew and by the start of the new year, I was pacing to make 4-figures in revenue per month. Might I remind you that this is money outside of my regular job?

My point isn't to share my side hustle income or make you think that things happen overnight without work. My point is to show that if you just start using your skills and talents and put a price tag on them, you too can generate another stream of income.

In 2018, I interviewed Valencia Morton—a single mother of one who was able to pay off $43,000 in debt with the money made from her side hustles. If that doesn't encourage you to use your gifts to generate additional income, I don't know what will.

Turn Your Side Hustle Into A Business

You don't have to have a registered business to start a side hustle; however, you will need to be a business if you plan on growing. With the help of the Internet, you can literally start a business in as little as 10 minutes.

Once you've proven your side hustle out—meaning you've actually made money from your product or services—it's time to make it an official legal entity. That means registering as a business entity with your state.

There are many ways that you can register a business. If you're doing the business alone, you can register your business as a Sole Proprietorship or as a Limited Liability Company. Partnerships and corporations are also business structures that may be fitting for your specific needs as well. You can find information on how to form your business on the IRS' business website or the equivalent government site for businesses for those outside of the United States.

Nonetheless, once you've done your research and decided what kind of entity your business should be registered as, you can simply register on your state's business registration website—which should end in .gov.

Follow the guides on the site to determine what information is needed to register and how much it costs.

Here's a general outline of the steps that you'll need to take to get your business up and running:

- ❑ Decide on a business name and ensure it isn't already trademarked or taken

- ❑ Secure website domain, email address, and social media accounts with business name (ex. GirlTalkwithFo.com and @GirlTalkwithFo on all social media)

- ❑ Register your business with your state (ex. Girl Talk with Fo, LLC)

- ❑ Acquire any necessary licenses, such as a retail/wholesale license

- ❑ Acquire an EIN number for your business from the IRS website

- ❑ Open a business bank account using your EIN number

Once you've taken these simple steps, you've got yourself a business!

Of course, you'll need to do your due diligence to maintain your business, including things like paying your business taxes and managing your business finances separate from your personal finances.

You may find that your business begins to take on a life of its own and starts to generate enough money to leave your traditional job. If this is the case, I encourage you to make the decision that works best for you and is aligned with your purpose.

Not everyone is created to be an entrepreneur, but everyone can create multiple streams of income.

Chapter 8: Manage Your Money

The truth is that anyone can make money. Anyone, in their right mind can get a job and exchange their service and time for money; however, it takes a dedicated person to manage their money.

There are tons of people who work hours upon hours and bring in a substantial amount of money, but have absolutely nothing to show for it. The issue that most people run into with money is typically not making it, but managing it.

I once read an alarming statistic citing that 70% of lottery winners end up being broke. I also watched a documentary showing the staggering number of professional athletes who endure the same fate after retirement.

These people didn't have a problem acquiring money, but they sure did have an issue of managing and keeping it.

But why? How can someone with so much money lose it all?

I'd venture to say that this happens every day to everyday people, just on a smaller scale. The average person won't amass millions of dollars overnight; however, the average person does the same job of losing the money that they do earn.

I'm not a psychologist or anything, but I've deduced two reasons that people who amass wealth tend to lose it quickly. The first is that they're stricken with a poverty mindset.

A poverty mindset is the mindset that says, *"I need to spend this and enjoy it because I never know when I'll have this opportunity again."* It's the mindset that is so accustomed to the struggle, that it doesn't know a life outside of it. Therefore, it'll cause you to self sabotage your way back into poverty.

The second reason is mismanagement. Afterall, if you've never had money to manage, how can you be successful at managing it overnight?

In 2018 a local resident in my city actually won the Mega Millions lottery. Not just the measly $1,000 lottery that at least one of our family members has won before. No! This person became a billionaire literally overnight—$1.5 billion to be exact.

I caught wind of it as I was driving by our local gas station one night. It was uncommonly crowded with news cameras and onlookers. After a quick Google search on my phone to see what was going on—because that's the world we live in—I discovered that the winning ticket had been purchased at that station.

Now, I've never played the lottery before, but that sure made me think about what I'd do if I had won.

My husband and I pondered the question, "What would we do if God blessed us with one billion dollars overnight?"

After we went through the usual process that we do with all of our money—tithe, save, invest, spend a little—we suddenly stopped in our tracks.

"Do banks even hold that much money? Are they insured for that? Where would we deposit it?" we rattled off.

We quickly learned that though we were great at managing money at our current level, we had no clue what to do beyond that. Our ignorance would likely put us in prime position to lose that money very quickly.

Money can come to anyone, but it will only stay with those who manage it well.

If you've ever had to ask yourself, *"Why am I always broke?"* the answer isn't that you can't make more money, because you can. The real answer is one that requires true introspection and honesty.

It's because you're a poor manager.

As much as I wanted to sugar coat that, for your sake, I couldn't. I was once a bad manager of money, too. I had to admit to myself that I had earned two great degrees and had landed a well paying job but I was terrible at managing the fruit of those accomplishments.

I had to admit that I had no idea how to budget, let alone stick to one. I had to admit that I spent money frivolously on things like hair and makeup. I had to admit that I had absolutely no idea what I was doing with the money that I was making.

After admitting those truths, I buckled down to change the narrative.

In order to get a grasp on how to manage money, I had to simplify it for myself. Those fluffy finance books weren't working for me, and they probably haven't worked for you either.

In my quest to learn and to, subsequently, teach others in a simplistic way, I was able to break down money management into three things.

Managing money consists of the following:

1. Saving
2. Sowing (Giving)
3. Spending

Think about it. Every time that you handle money, you're doing one of these three things. You're either saving it for something in the future, giving it away as a gift, or spending it on something. The key to managing your money well though, is making sure you have the right balance of these three things.

The unfortunate reality is that many people tend to do more of the spending than anything else and it becomes unbalanced. So, let's talk about how to effectively do all three.

If you want to have a great balance of each of these three things, there are two things that you need to do. First, you need to budget your money. Secondly, you need to make your saving, sowing, and spending automatic.

Budgeting

First, let's talk about budgeting. The dreaded "B" word. If you don't like the word budget, then call it a spending plan. Whatever you call it, remember that it's a tool and not a trap.

Before I get into the technicalities of creating a budget, I want to explore the definition of what a budget is.

According to Webster, a budget is a plan for the coordination of resources and expenditures. The operative word here is *plan*. So, to say that you're on a budget doesn't mean that you're being cheap or can't afford something. It merely means that you're on a plan. No matter how little you make, a budget is still necessary if you want to effectively manage your money.

Let me be clear about this, budget does not mean cheap!

I remember the first time that I tried (try may even be an overstatement) to get on the budget. I found a template online and attempted to fill out. I inputted what I was going to be making and the expenses that I thought I'd have.

Well . . . I was off . . . by a lot.

Not only was I off, but I also didn't have a plan for sticking with this said budget. It was just an idea, not a plan.

In order for a budget to actually be a plan for managing your money, it must be realistic and it must be a living document.

Many times, in our attempts to create what we think is a budget, we merely put unrealistic expectations on our spending. In theory, we believe that if we put a lower number than what we're currently spending on an expense, then we've put ourselves on a budget.

Budgeting is not putting an unrealistic, arbitrary number on a particular expense. A budget is taking into account what your income is, the necessary expenses you have, and creating a plan to manage your finances within your means.

Let's break down the three components of a budget.

1. Income

Your income is the most important line item of a budget. It's the maximum amount that you're able to spend within a given budgeting period. The first way that spending can get out of control and you can begin to accrue debt is when you don't understand this financial boundary.

It should go without saying, but your expenses should not surpass your income. When this happens, you are officially living outside of your means.

When creating a budget, you should only base what you're able to afford off of your consistent, "guaranteed" income. I put quotes because nothing is truly guaranteed, not even with a traditional job. That means, your budget should not be created based off of bonuses, overtime, or any other contingent income.

Many moons ago when I first started my career I worked in a manufacturing plant. Like most manufacturing environments, work was behind and overtime was a'plenty . . . until it wasn't. Very soon business wasn't doing so well and overtime was taken away.

The announcement wreaked havoc among many of the employees. I listened as husbands panicked about their ability to be able to keep up the payments for their large homes, boats, and cars that they had acquired with their overtime income. Like most Americans, they were living above their means—believing that the extra income would continue to flow.

Instead of creating a lifestyle off of the additional, contingent income, they should have kept their expenses under their base income amount. The extra income could have been used to pay off debt, their mortgage, put into savings, and/or invested.

Your expenses should not exceed your base income. So when creating a budget, the income that you need to know is your base income after taxes, also known as net income. Everything beyond that is extra that can be put toward your financial goals, such as paying off debt, saving, or investing.

2. Expected Expenses

Your expenses are the meat of the budget. After all, it's why you budget! You need to know where your income is being allocated.

The essence of budgeting is estimating how much these expenses will be during a given time period. For the most part, expenses tend to be the same every month or within a small deviation of an average.

The fact that this portion of your budget is titled "expected' expenses is indicative of one important thing—it should be reviewed before the expenses are incurred.

Remember, a budget is a plan and the true essence of a plan is that it is created before something happens. Each time you create a budget, you are creating a plan for your income to go toward expected expenses.

There are expenses that you will know the exact cost for each time they occur. For instance, you know what your phone bill will be each month. Likewise, you know how much you can expect to pay in rent or your mortgage as well. These things are consistent and do not change.

On the other hand, there are some expenses that you can't quite estimate exactly. Things like your groceries and utilities will vary each month. But, although you don't know what the exact amount will be, you can usually estimate these costs with historical data.

In cases like this, I recommend taking three months of expenses and finding the average of each category. You can expect that, unless you have a significant change to your lifestyle, these expenses will be within this range in the subsequent months.

3. Actual Expenses Incurred

Knowing and listing your income and your estimated expenses will mean absolutely nothing if you don't track your spending against this plan.

I like to say that a budget is a living document because you're always updating it. Now, I don't mean that you're updating your plan to allow for more spending. Instead, you're updating it to track your spending and to compare it to your plan.

Tracking your expenses as you incur them allows you to see how you're trending to your plan and make real time adjustment so that you don't go over it.

Again, without doing so, having a budget is pointless.

Think of your budget as a game plan. If you've ever played on a sports team, then you know that you don't enter into a competition without a game plan. It's devised based on your study of what's coming. In the case of sports, it's your opponent. For your budget, it's your expenses.

As the game is played you document performance and make adjustments. Within your budget, you'd document spending and make adjustments based on how close you are to reaching your budgeted amount.

There are several ways that you can make tracking your expenses easier. Though I prefer the more involved method of actually inputting expenses into a shared excel spreadsheet with my husband, there are apps that will automatically keep track of your expenses relative to your budget as soon as you swipe your debit card.

Apps To Track Your Expenses

Mint.com is a platform that I initially used to help track my debt payoff journey. In recent years, they've also developed an app that allows you to track your spending and it has the capability to automatically categorize your spending when it happens.

The EveryDollar Budgeting App is an app by Dave Ramsey that allows you to manage your budget from your phone. Like the Mint app, it also categorizes your spending for you.

Though I put a lot of emphasis on expenses, I'd like to make it clear that sowing, saving, and spending in general can all be categorized as expenses. They require that money be expended, therefore making them an expense. That means, just as your utilities and groceries are included in your budget, so should your sowing, saving, and discretionary spending outside of recurring expenses.

Sowing

The term sowing in finances is just another way to say giving. I prefer sowing because I am a firm believer that when you give, you're planting a seed that will reap a return for you in the future. Regardless of what you call it, it is still something that needs to be accounted for in your budget.

Though there is no limit on how much you should give, when it comes to budgeting, it should always be within your means and accounted for. My rule of thumb when it comes to sowing is to give at minimum 10% of my income. That's a tithe.

Many people handle their tithing differently; however, I like to give 10% of my *gross* income to my local church to help fund efforts in the community and abroad. This is the first expense that shows on our budget.

You may choose to give less or to give based on your net income. Either way, make sure that this is accounted for in your budget because it is an expense that should be planned for.

As an aside, I believe that giving should play a significant part in your personal finances. While on my debt free journey, I still gave. I believe that giving unlocks financial resources for you that you wouldn't have access to otherwise. I attribute my own financial success to managing well and giving.

SAVING

Much like sowing, saving is also an expense that needs to be planned for.

If you're working to get out of debt, this is something that you will pause until you've built up your initial $1,000 emergency fund. Otherwise, you'll add it as a line item in your budget as well.

There are three types of savings that you should consider. Those types are retirement savings, emergency savings, and savings for specific purchases. In general, you should save for large purchases, such as cars, homes, weddings, etc.

Again, there is no right answer for how much you should save; however there are rules of thumb. One of these is saving at least 10% toward your retirement. An easy formula that I like to use is sow 10%, save 10%, and live off (spend) the remaining 80%.

Of the three types of savings that you should have, I recommend putting money away into your retirement savings first. You can do this before you even get your paycheck, which doesn't require it being tracked on your budget.

How much you save after putting money away for retirement depends on your goals and your expenses. Obviously, you want to be able to still cover your necessary expenses and not just put all of your money away into savings.

Determine how much you can reasonably put way into savings each pay period while still managing your other expenses. This savings amount should be a line item in your budget that you handle like you would any other expense or payment that you have to make.

Spending

As I mentioned before, the majority of your finances will go toward spending if you're following the 10/10/80 percent breakdown of your finances. Your spending will encompass your expected expenses and is ultimately what the majority of your budget will consist of.

In order to manage your spending, you'll need visibility to your expenses. That's where zero-based budgeting comes into play.

How To Create A Zero-Based Budget

Now that you understand the basis of budgeting and the components of a budget, it's time to actually create one.

A zero-based budget is a budget that allocates every penny to a specific line item. By doing so, the amount of income coming in less your expected expense should equal zero.

$$Income - Expenses = \$0$$

This doesn't mean that you must spend every penny. It just means that every cent of your money will be applied to saving, sowing, or spending on expenses and debt repayment.

If you are creating a budget for the first time, there are seven steps that you'll need to follow in order to create one that's useable.

Step 1. Create a list of all of your monthly expenses.

Your list should be as exhaustive as possible to insure visibility to your spending. Below is an example of some items that may appear on your budget. There are things that you may spend money on every month and other things that are one offs, but still should be accounted for. It helps to break these expenses up into categories, because at the end of the year, you can see which category has the most spending. You can grab my monthly budget printable with these categories in the Everyday Chick's Guide to Money digital workbook.

<table>
<tr>
<td><u>Sowing</u>
Tithes
Charity</td>
<td><u>Saving</u>
Emergency Fund
College Fund
Other</td>
<td><u>Housing</u>
Mortgage/Rent
Repairs/Maintenance
HOA
Property Taxes</td>
</tr>
<tr>
<td><u>Utilities</u>
Electricity
Gas
Water
Trash
Phone/Mobile
Internet/Cable</td>
<td><u>Food</u>
Groceries
Dining Out</td>
<td><u>Clothing</u>
Adults
Children
Dry Cleaning/Alterations</td>
</tr>
<tr>
<td><u>Transportation</u>
Gas / Oil
Repairs /Tires
License / Taxes
Car Replacement</td>
<td><u>Medical/Health</u>
Medications
Doctor Bills
Dentist
Optometrist
Vitamins
Gym</td>
<td><u>Insurance</u>
Life Insurance
Health Insurance
Homeowner/Renters
Auto Insurance
Disability Insurance
Identity Theft
Long-Term Care</td>
</tr>
<tr>
<td><u>Personal</u>
Toiletries
Cosmetics
Books/Supplies
Subscriptions
Gifts
Pocket Money (His)
Pocket Money (Hers)</td>
<td><u>Recreation</u>
Entertainment
Vacation</td>
<td><u>Debts</u>
Car Payment 1
Car Payment 2
Credit Card 1
Credit Card 2
Credit Card 3
Student Loan 1
Student Loan 2</td>
</tr>
</table>

Step 2. Get an average for each of these expenses over three months.

Use your bank statement to average out how much you've spent on each item over a three month period. This is how much you can expect to pay for this expense again in the future.

You'll find that most items should be the same over the course of those months. Items like rent and debt repayments should not change; however, you may find a range for things like groceries and utility bills. The purpose is to get a number that represents what you can expect to pay for each of these expenses in the future.

Step 3. Calculate the total cost of these expenses.

Once you have an average cost for each of these recurring items, it's time to add them up to get a total of what your monthly expenses are. This is the amount that you need have in your bank account each month to be able to cover your cost of living.

Step 4. Compare your expenses to your total monthly income.

Now that you know exactly how much your expenses are each month, you need to ensure that you actually have enough to cover those expenses. Your next step is to compare your net income—income after taxes, healthcare, and other expenses taken out of your paycheck—to the total expenses that you incur each month.

For many people, the expenses will be greater than their income. This is an indication that you're spending above your means and need to find ways to cut your monthly expenses.

Some common expenses that can be reduced or eliminated include:

- Cable
- Eating out
- Nail and hair appointments
- Groceries
- Gym membership
- Unused subscription services

Step 5. Create a revised list of expenses.

Once you've identified areas that you can cut back on or remove, create a new list of your expenses reflecting the reduced amount that you plan to spend in those categories.

This will become your budget. It is essentially your expense plan for the month and your aim is to spend no more than the amount that you've listed, or allocated, for each expense listed.

Step 6. Track expenses.

Now that you've established your budget, you must keep track of your expenses. Each time you make a payment or purchases, document how much you've spent. Though I suggest doing this manually starting out as a way to ensure that you're constantly looking at your budget, you can leverage the apps previously mentioned to do this automatically.

Step 7. Make adjustments.

As you track your spending, you should be taking note of how much you have left to spend in that particular category. For instance, if your dining out budget is $50 and by the first weekend of the month you've spent $40, you know that you need to start cooking for the rest of the month to avoid going over your budget.

Ultimately, your budget should be a guide to your spending. It doesn't do the work for you, so saying that budgeting doesn't work for you really means that you aren't disciplined around sticking to your plan.

When it comes to budgeting, I have a few rules that you should follow.

Rules of Budgeting

1. You must complete your budget before you get paid. That's the only way this thing works. Plan your spending before you spend. Know where your money is going to go before it comes to you.

2. Update it frequently. This means adding expenses as they are made. It does not mean tweaking the budget to give yourself more money.

3. If you're married, budget *with* your spouse. Money is a leading cause of divorce. Get on the same page about how you will spend your money.

Budgeting For Monthly Or Inconsistent Income

Not everyone gets paid a consistent income or every two weeks. In fact, when I changed businesses within my career, I shifted from a biweekly paycheck to only getting paid monthly. In this scenario, my husband and I really had to be diligent about how we budgeted.

Because this may be your case, I'll share how I've managed instances of monthly income and how you can manage inconsistent, commission based income.

Monthly Income

Although you may get paid on a monthly basis, I still recommend using the aforementioned method and budgeting on a biweekly basis.

Using the same exercise outlined previously, you'll need to list out your expenses and determine which bills fall into the beginning of the month (the 1st-15th) and what falls into the latter part of the month (the 16th-31st.) If you find that you're heavier with bills on one half of the month versus the other, just change your bill statement date to help even it out.

Arrange to have your paycheck deposited into a savings account. This is the only case that I recommend using a savings account that is attached to your checking account. This account will hold your funds until they are transferred into your checking account to cover your expenses for that half of the month. It should be an account that will not penalize you for a zero balance.

You'll set up your bank account to auto transfer half of your paycheck from that savings account on the 1st of the month and the second half on the 15th of the month. You're essentially simulating getting paid twice a month.

You'll budget for expenses happening in the first half of the month, and before the second transfer happens, you'll budget for expenses in the second half of the month.

With this method, you should only be making two transfers per month out of your savings account. This is important because the US government limits you to six transfers per month from your savings account.

Inconsistent Income

If you're an entrepreneur or work on commission, then your income is likely inconsistent. In this case, you're typically unable to predict the amount of money that will come in each month. Instances like this will require you to be even more reliant on a budget.

You'll begin by following the same steps outlined before. You'll list all of your expenses that you have every month; however, for your expected income, you'll use the lowest income that you've received in the past year as your baseline. This will allow you to budget for the worst case scenario.

Beside each line item, you'll place a number indicating which expense is a priority. For instance, your mortgage may be number one, while entertainment may be 30. In general, you should prioritize shelter, food, and transportation first.

Each time you get paid, you'll use your income to cover each item by priority. For example, you'd put money toward your mortgage first and apply anything left ot the next expense in the priority list.

Since you are using the lowest income amount as your baseline, you'll likely get income above that amount. In such case, you'll list it as additional income, but still continue to cover expenses based on your priority list.

If you have funds left over after all expenses are paid, you may use the extra money to apply toward debt, saving, or for discretionary spending.

Updating Your Budget

I'll reiterate the fact that the budget is indeed a living document. That means you need to update it consistently. That's where your budgeting meetings comes into play.

Your budget meeting is where you sit down to review your budget for the upcoming pay period. It's a time to see how you've spent over the last pay period. If you have any additional money, that can be used to put toward debt or savings, and to create a plan for the coming pay period.

I advise conducting your budget meeting biweekly and no less than a day before you get paid. Waiting until you get paid to tell your money where to go is a disaster waiting to happen.

When you conduct your budget meeting, you'll need to have a calendar nearby. This is important because you want to set aside money in your budget for any upcoming events like birthdays, weddings, baby showers, etc. These things shouldn't be a surprise to you, so account for them ahead of time. Otherwise, you'll end up spending money that you hadn't planned on spending and going over your budget.

If you're married, this is something that I recommend doing with your spouse. Money should be managed together within a marriage and not separately. If you can sit down with your spouse to plan out where your money is going, you've avoided one of the leading causes of divorce.

Once you have created your budget and made the necessary adjustments to stay within your means, it's time to automate your money to do exactly what you plan it to do.

Automating your finances simply means putting your savings, sowing, and spending on autopilot so that you don't have to rely on your memory or self discipline.

If you haven't figured it out already, the key to both getting out of debt and building your bank is discipline. But, we're human. And, as much as we like to think that we won't eat the donut in the break room, most of us don't have the discipline not to.

The same is true with money. Although we say we won't spend that money, if it's not put away, we will. That's where automating your finances comes into play.

What To Automate In Your Finances

Not only are humans creatures of habit, but we also like to take the path of least resistance. So, when you think about money management, you want to make it as easy as possible. There are a plethora of apps and websites that allow you to play that human tendency to your advantage by automating your finances.

Retirement Savings

Putting your money away for your retirement investing can be easily automated. To do so, you can have your employer automatically deduct it from your paycheck. Each time you get paid, this money will automatically come out of your check and into your account. It's amazing how much you won't miss it when you never see it. This is usually what people mean when they tell you to pay yourself first. It's putting money away for your future.

General Savings

There may be some things outside of your retirement that you'd like to save for. It could be a vacation, a car, or even a house. Whatever it is, you can automate your finances to save for this every time you get paid.

Again, if you're paying off debt, I recommend pausing any savings efforts outside of first funding your emergency account. But, once you're out of debt, you should begin putting money away for large purchases.

There are two ways that I recommend for automating your savings, both of which I've tried and have found success with. The first approach is to have a portion of your paycheck directly deposited into your savings account when you get paid. If your employer is up to date with their payment system, this shouldn't be an issue.

Just arrange to have a certain percentage or dollar amount deposited to a savings account every time you get paid. You won't have to worry about transferring the money, which means you won't forget. And, because it's not going to your checking account, you won't even miss the money.

Another option is to have your bank automatically transfer the money 2-3 days after your direct deposit clears in your checking account. In this case, all money will initially go to the same account, but after a few days, your bank will automatically transfer the specified funds into a connected savings account.

This is the best approach if your employer doesn't have the capability to split up your paycheck among different accounts; however, if you lack self-discipline, I wouldn't advise it. That's because if you don't ever see the money in your account, there is no temptation to spend it.

Some banks offer incentives when you automatically transfer money from your checking to your savings account; however, this usually requires that your savings account be with the same bank, which I don't recommend.

Bill Payments

If you've ever been late paying a bill when you've had the money to pay it, automating your payments is probably a great option for you.

When I was single, I had all of my bill payments automated. I did this for two reasons:

1. I'd sometimes forget to pay a bill
2. My student loan company reduced my interest rates

As adamant as we can be about paying our bills on time, we're human and sometimes we just forget. That's why I suggest automating your bill payments. This allows you to ensure that your payments are made on time and that you don't forget.

Much like automatically transferring money from your checking to savings account has its incentive, so does automating some of your bill payments.

In my case, automating my student loan payments actually saved me a fraction of a percentage on my loan. Though it may not seem like much, I was looking for any available way to save money on my student loans. So, it may be advantageous for you to also automate your payments.

Worried about not having enough funds? If you get paid biweekly, there's always the case where your first paycheck may not cover all of your bills that fall within the two week period. That's not uncommon. In this case, many companies allow you to change your billing date.

For instance, if your bills for the first two weeks of the month equal $2,000, but you're only making $1,500, you can move your billing date for your cell phone, Internet, etc. The first time you do this, it may cost you a bit more just to make up for the days that would've been covered if you paid sooner. After that, you should be good to go.

If this is the case for you, talk to your service provider to see if you can move your billing date to the latter part of the month.

What Bank Accounts To Have

In 2018, I wrote a blog post on the number of bank accounts that adults should have. Based on the feedback that I received, it's clear that many people still think that all you need is one checking account and one savings account.

If you have at least those two, good for you. That's the first step in managing your money; however, you'll need more. In order to effectively manage your money, you have to be able to see it clearly. That means, it needs to be organized.

Think about it. Would you put all of your clothes—underwear, socks, work clothes, gym clothes, etc.—in one drawer? No! You wouldn't be able to find what you need efficiently and it'd just be a hot mess.

Instead, you separate your clothes out. You may even hang them up by category and color like I do. It's all about being able to see and find what you need quickly.

The same is true for your finances. You need to be able to see and find what you need quickly. That's why just having one checking account and one savings account doesn't work. How do you know what money is allocated for your vacation savings versus your car and vice versa?

At a minimum, I recommend having five bank accounts, all for different uses. I learned a long time ago that if you can name what you're saving for, you're more likely to actually save for it. So, if you have at least five different accounts for five specific reasons, you're more likely to put money away and manage it better.

Here are the five accounts that I recommend having:

1. General Checking

This one should probably go without saying, but you're definitely going to need a general checking account. If you don't have a separate account just for paying bills, this would be it. You general checking account is what I call your "home" account. It's the account that you'll have your paycheck deposited to and the account that you'll ultimately transfer money out of to other accounts.

Most banks have free online checking accounts that you can easily access online or locally. Unlike a savings account, I recommend using a bank that has a local branch that you can visit if necessary. There's no advantage in using an online bank in this case, as you're not earning any interest from this account. The point here is convenience and the ability to access your funds.

2. Emergency Fund

Apart from your "home" checking account, having an emergency fund account is the next most important thing to have.

An emergency fund should be held in a high yield savings account and typically accounts for 6-12 months of your expenses. The intent of this account is to be a cushion in case an emergency happens and you need large sums of money fast.

Your emergency fund should be held in a bank that's separate from your general checking account to avoid the temptation of withdrawing from it unnecessarily. In the case of an emergency, you should be able to access these funds by transferring them into your main checking account—usually taking 1-3 business days or using a bank issued card.

If you're working to build up your emergency fund, saving 6-12 months of expenses should be your target for this account; however, if you're currently paying off debt, $1,000 is a reasonable amount to cover emergencies.

3. General Savings

A general savings account is much different from your emergency fund. This account is intended to hold funds for general items that you may be saving up for.

General savings is ideal for having funds readily available for Christmas and/or birthdays. It's an account that can be used for anything that's not an emergency, but would require that you save up a bit of cash.

Though I recommend creating a specific account for large purchases, like a car, this account could very well be used for that purpose and many more. In fact, I've known single friends to use this account to save for a one-day engagement ring and wedding.

Much like the emergency fund though, there should be limits on accessing these funds. Only use it when you're ready to make a purchase that you've intentionally saved up for.

4. Travel Account

As much as I enjoy traveling, I enjoy it even more when it's debt free. That's where a travel account comes into play.

The travel account is intended for use as implied—to travel. No more using the credit card to book your stay, this checking account is designed for you to stash your vacation cash.

Why checking instead of savings? Because you'll need a card to hold your reservations and book your flights.

Reserving an account just for traveling puts it at the forefront of your savings goals. No more missing out on travel opportunities or getting in debt when you've been putting money away each time you get paid.

5. Home Repair/Decor

Every homeowner knows that there comes a time when something will go wrong with their home.

Whether it's an air conditioner going out, a pipe bursting, or a leaky roof—there will always be something to fix. That's why having a home repair account is so clutch. Imagine not having to dip into your emergency fund or savings to pay for that overpriced repair.

Better yet, how about already having money stashed away from those much needed renovations and decor upgrades.

Where To Bank

Where you choose to bank is another important factor in managing your money. Afterall, you want to make sure that your money is in the right hands. At the end of the day, though all banks do the same thing—hold and insure your money—all banks are not created equal.

I first learned this when I moved to Houston, TX for my first job. In the midst of moving, I realized that the local bank that I used in college (only because they gave $10 for opening an account) was not available in the city. I immediately had to switch to a bank that I could access going forward.

No big deal, right? At the time it wasn't, but it showed me that local banks wouldn't be a viable option if I continued to move, which I did.

Years later, I discovered the phenomenon of online banking.

I'd see commercials boasting high APY, but I had no clue what it meant. With some research, I discovered that it meant high annual percentage yield—meaning, you get a lot of interest back (aka free money) on the money you put in the account.

At the time, these online accounts required a credit check, but now they're commonplace and how I choose to bank.

Online banking can seem scary for some people because you can't actually go into a bank. But, let's be real. When is the last time that you've actually gone inside of a bank?

If not the ATM, you've probably made use of their online banking options.

The benefits of online banking are that you can access it 24/7, they're easy to open, and they typically have little to no fees. When you're comparing different banks, here are a few things that you need to consider.

1. Ease of opening and accessing account

Everything is about ease and convenience these days. Opening a bank account is no different.

Would it surprise you to know that I haven't been inside of an actual bank in over a year? And the only reason I went a year ago was because I needed a cashier's check to make the down payment on our home. Not surprisingly, it'd been over a year before then for my last visit to join accounts with my husband.

With everything at the touch of our fingertips, I find no need to go into a brick and mortar bank for my transactions. That's why I prefer a savings account that I can open and access without the hassle of having to find time to go to a branch.

When considering which savings account to use, I recommend considering online savings accounts for their shear ease and convenience. Online banking gives you the option of being able to access your accounts anywhere and typically come with 24/7 support via phone or chat.

Online banks also have the advantage of offering higher interest rates, because they don't carry the overhead and expenses of maintaining a brick and mortar branch.

2. Minimum balance required and fees

I'm all about saving the coins, especially when it comes to fees. So, when considering a bank account, the minimum balance amount and associated fees is of utmost importance.

Some banks assess fees for your account being below a specific balance. This is important if you are using your savings account to stash for a trip or to make big purchases, where funds will ultimately be coming out.

If you know that your account may fall under that minimum balance, it's wise to avoid it and find a bank that doesn't assess fees. There are a few banks that offer minimal to no balance requirements.

3. Annual Percentage Yield (APY)

Admittedly, APY may be the single most deciding factor when I'm accessing a potential savings account. Why? Because it's free money!

An accounts APY is the amount of interest that you will receive each year on the money held in your account. For example, if your accounts APY is 1.85%, that means you'll receive $1.85 for every $100 in your account that year.

So, imagine how much interest you can gain from having 6-12 months of an emergency fund in the right account!

Before you get too excited, know that the government will get their portion in taxes from the interest earned. If your account earns interest over a certain amount, you'll have to submit at 1099-INT form to the IRS reporting your income from interest.

Now that you've gotten a handle on managing your money, you have the foundation to start multiplying. Let's build wealth!

Chapter 9: Multiply Your Money

This is where the fun comes in. It's where wealth is built and your money begins to work for you—multiplying your money.

After all is said and done and you've worked hard for your money, it's time for your money to start working for you. The phrase, "let your money work for you," just means let your money make money for you.

But how exactly does money make money? Through compound interest and investments.

Have you ever heard of the phrase, "The rich are getting richer?" Well it's the simple concept of multiplying money that makes this statement true. If you can get your finances to the point where your money begins to make money, you'll be among the wealthy.

Multiplying your money is how wealth is built.

In the *Dump Your Debt* section of this book, I explained how lenders profit from the interest that you pay on debt. It's how they make their money. So, imagine if you leveraged that same concept for your personal finances.

Essentially, you leverage the phenomenon of interest to allow your money to grow without you having to lift a finger.

Getting to this point in your finances isn't as hard as you think. In fact, you can start now by simply putting your money in the right place. You may be building wealth now without even knowing it.

Here are the four major ways that you can allow your money to begin working for you:

Leveraging A High APY Savings Account

Utilizing a high APY savings account is the simplest, and least risky way, to multiply your money. Hence me being so adamant about it in the prior chapters.

If you're going to be putting your money away in a savings account, you may as well let it collect interest so that you can make money from it. It's the simplest form of wealth building that you can do right now.

This is perfect for your emergency fund that will be holding at least 6-12 months worth of expenses. Having large amounts of money collecting interest is a quick way to grow your money overtime. It's literally just sitting there growing.

So, if you didn't open a high APY savings account in the earlier chapter, take a moment to do so now!

Don't get discouraged if you're only making a few cents in the beginning. As you begin to build your account, those cents turn into dollars, then even more dollars. At some point, you may be able to use that interest to invest—an even greater form of letting your money work for you!

Retirement Savings

Your retirement savings account is another way that your money is working for you. It's allowing your money to grow through diversified mutual funds, bonds, stocks, CDs, etc. As the market improves, so will your earnings.

The average return for the US stock market is around 10%. That means over time, if you continue to invest money without touching it, not only will your principal investment grow 10%, but you'll get a return on the money that you continued to put into your account.

The growth of your retirement fund relies on you not touching it. That means not taking out a 401(k) loan to put a down payment on a home or for an emergency. Your retirement account should be a set it and forget it matter, only making adjustments to your portfolio as your become more risk averse with age.

There are several options for retirement savings, all of which can be explored in more detail on the *IRS.gov* website; however, I'll give you a general overview of your options here. In each case, the IRS limits the amount of money that can be placed in these accounts each year and there are variations to how the funds can be taxed.

401(k)

The 401(k) is one of the five employer-sponsored retirement plans available to date. In most cases, the employer matches your contribution and there are requirements on what age funds must be deducted. Take advantage of this to put as much away early on as you can. The longer your money has time to grow, the more you'll have in the future.

Individual Retirement Arrangements (IRAs)

If you're self employed, a stay at home spouse, or if you've maxed out your 401(k), you can arrange your own retirement account with a bank, brokerage firm, or other financial institution that holds investments. There are currently two types of IRAs that you can choose from—either Roth or Traditional. The difference is how and when you will be taxed on the funds in the account.

Investing In The Stock Market

Another way to multiply your money is through investing in the stock market, apart from your retirement. Where some retirement accounts may be limited in what you can add to your portfolio, you have the freedom to invest as you please outside of these accounts.

There are many schools of thought when it comes to investing. Some people prefer curating a portfolio of shares from their own hand picked companies like Apple, Google, Amazon, Facebook, and other well performing entities. Others may find funds or cryptocurrency to be more viable options. There is an endless sea of opportunity when you enter the world of investing.

If you're ready to start investing, I recommend reading *The Sassy Investor* written by Michelle Hung. This is a great, easy to understand resource that breaks down investing and what you should do to begin. You can access this book in the Everyday Chick's Guide to Money digital workbook.

Real Estate Investing

Real estate investing is the bread and butter of wealth generation. Owning land and property that has value and can be rented for passive income is the quickest way to see your money multiplied.

For a long time, the barrier of entry into real estate investing was high. Only those who had accumulated wealth by other means could afford to get into this market; however, the times have changed and the average person can start investing in real estate today.

In 2018, I interviewed Kendra Barnes of the Key Resource—an online platform teaching everyday young adults how to start real estate investing. By age 30, she owned seven rental properties and was bringing in over $150,000 in rental income per year!

But here's the kicker . . . Kendra didn't have money or properties passed down to her. She merely played a game about real estate investing, found enough money for a down payment, and started building her real estate empire.

Her story—among many others that I've heard over the years—goes to show that you can start building wealth today through real estate investing. It's not just for the uber wealthy and those on HGTV, it's for the everyday chick as well.

If you want to find out more about investing in real estate and how you can literally start with zero dollars, check out Kendra's course, which you can access within the Everyday Chick's Guide to Money digital workbook.

Buying A Home Without Credit

Earlier in the book, I mentioned that it is possible to buy a home without having credit. As promised, I'll tell you how.

When my husband and I were on the market for our first home, we knew that we would take out a mortgage. Although we could have spent a few more years saving to pay for a home cash, we decided this was the best option for our situation.

Because we were debt free, we knew that credit would be an issue. Afterall, your credit history and credit score are how lenders determine what they'll approve and what your interest rate will be. Ultimately, my husband had a low credit score because he had paid off his student loans five years prior and hadn't used debt since.

On the other hand, I did have a high credit score because I had a long history from paying off my student loans and because I had owned a credit card. But, if we were to spend months looking for a home before buying, I'd be in the same situation as him. I'd have a long break in credit activity and my score would drop drastically.

We had two options in this situation. We could play the system by getting a credit card, using it to make small purchases, and immediately paying it off to raise my husband's score and to keep mine high. Or, we could use manual underwriting.

Manual underwriting is a manual process that lenders undertake to evaluate your ability to pay back a loan. This is contrary to the automated process that is widely used. Though manual underwriting is a bit more tedious, it allows you to get financing without having to use ongoing credit or worry about your FICO® Score.

To go through the manual underwriting process, you will have to provide documentation that will show proof of consistent payments. Things like rent, cell phone, and utility payments are all forms of documentation that can support your history of consistent payments. Basically, you're manually showing your credit history as opposed to having a score that quickly validates it.

Because this is such a manual process, you may imagine that not many lenders want to take it on. Afterall, it's more work and time for them. Nonetheless, there are still some lenders who support the debt and credit score free life who will take you through the process. The most noted lender specializing in manual underwriting is Churchill Mortgage.

After weighing the option of manual underwriting and "playing" the system, I'll admit that we did the latter. We opened the most basic credit card account, used it to raised our scores, and closed out the account some time after we closed on the home.

In general, this isn't something that I would recommend, especially if you don't have the discipline necessary to manage a credit card and close it out. In hindsight, we could have leveraged manual underwriting and it would have taken the same amount of time as "playing" the system. Going forward though, we fully intend on paying for our future homes in cash.

With that being said, we are working diligently to pay off our home to become completely debt free (again) in the next four years. This means, we will have paid off our 15-year mortgage in just six years.

Though less aggressive than our initial quest to becoming debt free, we are still leveraging the principles outlined in this book.

CHAPTER 10: LEAVE A LEGACY

There's no doubt in my mind that if you start applying these four tools for multiplying your money and using the resources recommended, you'll have a net worth that you never imagined having.

At the time of this book being written, my husband and I have employed all but real estate investing, which we plan to do once we've paid off our first home. At that point, our plan is to pay for our subsequent properties with cash!

Building wealth is great, but you must remember that it's not just about you. Way back in the first section of this book, we identified money as just a tool. It's a tool to provide a better life for you and your family. So, I don't teach these things so that you can go out and collect material things and have houses for the sake of having them. Instead, I want you to leverage these tools to build wealth that can be passed on for generations.

Let's close this thing out by talking about generational wealth,

GENERATIONAL WEALTH

Over the past few years, I've found the term generational wealth to be a bit of a buzzword. Among minority communities, grassroots efforts are taking place to educate people on what it means to leave a financial legacy to future generations and rightfully so.

Minority communities have long been disadvantaged when it comes to wealth building. Laws were created that prevented the ability to purchase land, homes, and to find careers that offered a better quality of life. Though things are not perfect or solved, there is still opportunity to build wealth and make the future brighter for our families.

That's why I wrote this book.

I remember sitting in my office one afternoon reflecting on the sacrifices and advancements that my ancestors have made that enable me to even write this book from the perspective of someone who is building generational wealth.

I thought about my great grandfather and the stories that my grandmother has shared.

He was a farmer in rural South Carolina. And despite segregation and laws established to prevent him from advancing, he did—in an incredible way.

My great grandfather wasn't just a farmer, but he was a farmer who owned the land that his crops were grown on. In fact, as my grandmother tells it, he even paid off the land early. Because of him, that land still remains in our family. Acres upon acres of land purchased by a man who was denied equal education and opportunity.

Though I never met him, I appreciate the foundation and mindset that he left for me and my family. If a black man in the south during the early 1900s can begin leaving a legacy for his family, so can you.

A part of leaving a legacy is ensuring that you protect what you've built.

We've seen it way too many times over the years where celebrities have built wealth and financial empires, yet did nothing to protect it or pass it down upon their death. Such behavior is irresponsible and downright selfish.

Building wealth is only one half of the equation. The other component is protecting it such that it can be a legacy.

There are a few critical things that you need to include in your personal finance management in order to do so. Let's explore these things.

Filing System

Let's start with the most basic form of protecting your legacy that you can implement today. That's a basic storage and filing system for your important financial documents.

Organization is key when it comes to managing your finances and leaving a legacy. That's why I suggest getting a water and fireproof filing box for these documents. This is something that is protected, but can be accessed by your family in case of an emergency.

Create sections labeled as follows:

Financial Documents

- Receipts
- Tax Documents
- Mortgage/Rent Documents
- Paystubs
- Charitable Giving Records

Health Documents

- Medical Records
- Health Insurance Documents
- Life Insurance Policies

Legal Documents

- Estate Plan/Will/Power Attorney
- Marriage License
- Passports
- Social Security Cards
- Birth Certificates
- Voter Registration

Simply organizing your financial and life affair documents can make a tremendous difference. In addition to putting them in a safe storage system, be sure to also put it in a discrete location and have it locked.

If you're married, your spouse should have access to this file and know where things are. You should also appoint an emergency contact who will have information on how to access this information in case of an emergency.

This brings up an important point. You need to appoint people in your life who can act on your behalf in case of any emergency. These are the people who should be appointed in your estate plan.

Estate Plan

No one wants to talk about dying, but the reality is that every one of us is appointed a time to leave this earth. Knowing this should give you even more reason to make sure your affairs are in order when that time comes.

I've lived through my share of deaths within my family in a short lifespan. I've been in the funeral homes planning homegoing services. I've also been in the family rooms where discussions are being had about what was left to whom and what was promised, but not written down.

No family should have to make important decisions during grief. Thoughts are irrational and emotions are high. That's why it's necessary to have an estate plan.

An estate plan isn't just for the uber wealthy. If you're a living, breathing adult, you should have one.

In 2018, I sat down with my own personal attorney and also interviewed Attorney Jehan Crump-Gibson to get more information on this subject. What I found was that despite the myths that exist around estate planning, the necessary documents that are needed are quite simple to have filed.

Let me address these myths.

Myth 1: Only The Wealthy Need An Estate Plan
Estate plans don't have a minimum net worth requirement. Just because you aren't wealthy doesn't mean that your assets don't deserve to be legally protected upon your death. Whatever you have, make sure you have a plan for it after you die. Whether it's to family or a charity, make sure those left behind know where you want your money to go so that they can honor your wishes.

Myth 2: Estate Plans Are For The Elderly
The truth is, estate planning isn't just for the more mature in age. If you are 18 years old, meaning you're legally an adult, you need to leave instructions about more things than just money. Things like:

- *Who acts on your behalf in the event that you're incapacitated?*
- *Who handles your finances if you're unable to?*
- *Who gets your possessions when you pass away?*

Don't assume that your parents will do all of these things for you. This is especially critical when you'd prefer one parent to handle your matters over another. You're never too young to have a plan in place just in case.

Myth 3: My Spouse Or Parent Will Automatically Get Everything
Assumptions always get you. This one may cost you and your family. Though being married has its inherent legal rights, it is important to ensure that all assets are titled and legally arranged to be given to your spouse. You'll also need a plan in case the both of you pass simultaneously.

As for parents, each state's laws differ when it comes to determining how property will be distributed when there is no will. Don't leave this to chance or state.

Myth 4: I Can Draft One Myself And Keep It With My Files
There is no law against drafting your own will. In fact, there are tons of websites that provide templates for you based on your state of residence. However, after speaking with my personal attorney and realizing the many nuances involved, I'd recommend working with a professional.

I'll be honest, working with an attorney does come with a cost; however, it also comes with peace of mind that your estate matters are being handled properly and all bases are covered. *And, let's be real . . .* If you were going to draft one yourself, you would've done it already.

As you think about things to save up for, make your estate plan one of those things. Work with an attorney who can write a plan that can capture all of your life changes. Take a moment to revisit it at the start of every year and make note of any life changes that have taken place that would require your documents to be updated.

As your family begins to grow and you have children, review these documents with them. As morbid as it may sound, they'll need to know what's going to happen upon your death.

Quite frankly, their inheritance shouldn't be a secret. Get it all out in the air while you're alive so that there are no issues or misunderstandings upon your death. Nothing can be debated when its written, notarized, and explained while you're living.

Drafting an estate plan will require an honest assessment of the people in your life. You'll need to know who will take care of your children, who will disperse assets, or who will make medical decisions if you're incapacitated. It makes you take an honest look at your circle and really determine how much you trust the people closest to you.

Estate planning also forces you to have honest and tough conversations with your family. Trust me, it's not fun asking a family member to take care of your children in the case of your untimely death. But, it's one of those life conversations that need to happen.

Life Insurance

Each year, without fail, I see a post float across my social media account with someone requesting funds to pay for funeral expenses for a loved one.

It's sad, but also irresponsible. No adult should be without life insurance unless they have the financial means in liquid assets to pay for the cost of burial expenses and to cover the lost income that their family will experience. That's being self-insured.

Most people don't meet that criteria of being self-insured, which means that at some point, everyone needs coverage.

The earlier in life that you can get life insurance coverage, the better. You're at a much lower risk of illness and death when you're younger, making the rates a lot lower. Essentially, you want to lock in a much lower rate earlier on and be covered for either your whole life or for term that you choose.

As you get older, you run a much higher risk of being uninsurable. Many companies will not insure those with pre-existing conditions that would put them at a higher risk for dying, and subsequently, requiring them to pay out a claim.

I remember when my parents got life insurance. It was a little later in life for them, but they got it nonetheless.

A few months after my parents got coverage, my father was diagnosed with stage 3 pancreatic cancer.

He literally got covered in the nick of time, only by God's grace. He's an exception. Most people don't get as "lucky" and are left footing expensive medical bills and subsequent burial costs.

Though they were older when they got coverage, their diligence in getting it done saved my family from what could have been an extreme financial burden.

The point is that you need to get coverage as soon as you can. You never know what curve balls life will throw, so at least mitigate the financial risk.

PROFESSIONALS

It's inevitable that at some point in your financial journey, your ability to manage will grow beyond you. At this point, you'll need to start enlisting help in the form of professionals. Now, this doesn't mean that you completely turn your finances over to them without the slightest clue as to what they're doing. Instead, it means partnering with them to ensure that you're making the best decisions for your financial present and future.

As a general rule of thumb, I recommend having three professionals on your team. Your team should consist of an insurance agent, attorney, and an accountant.

Insurance Agent

Typically, you don't think of an insurance agent as someone that you'll need to help manage your finances; however, I believe that they play an important role in protecting your assets. They're the ones who will help you find the right insurance coverage for your vehicle, home, and business.

Though you may not see them as frequently as the other professionals, having someone you trust who can grow with you through your different life phases can make things easier when it's time to change coverage.

Growing up, my parents leveraged this practice. Even to this day, my mom can hop on the phone with her insurance agent to ask questions or make changes based on life events with no issue. Her agent knows her, her situation, and can make recommendations for her specific needs. There's peace of mind in knowing that you're just a phone call away from having your questions answered.

Getting Christmas cards and random gifts are an added benefit as well!

Attorney

Attorneys aren't just for criminal cases and settling disputes. You'll need an attorney to draft your estate plan and will, and for general counsel.

Having an attorney on retainer, or basically paying to reserve their time every month, isn't necessary for what you'll need; however, having an attorney that you have identified as someone you can approach for counsel is important. In this case, you'd just schedule services as needed and pay their required fee.

I recommend finding an attorney who can grow with you and your family and also has the heart of a teacher. There's no right or wrong way to find one, but asking lots of questions can allow you to sift through your options.

My husband and I found our attorney via Google. While attempting to find someone to draft up our will and estate plan, we searched, called, and emailed several attorneys in our area. We took note of how they responded (or if they responded), their willingness to assist us, and of course, their fee.

By simply asking questions and observing, we were able to find an attorney who fits us. Someone who we would trust with our future legal questions and matters, someone who teaches us, and someone who looks out for our best interest. Take the time to find an attorney who can do the same for you.

Accountant

The last professional that I'd recommend keeping in your professional arsenal is an accountant. This is the person who will make sure that you're paying the right amount of taxes, and if you have a business, that you're managing your business finances correctly as well.

Unlike the others, you will likely see your accountant on a more consistent basis, perhaps quarterly.

In addition to an accountant, you may also see an advice-only financial advisor. This will be someone who can take an unbiased look at your financial goals and determine if you're on the right track. They'll have no vested interest in you investing a certain way or using their service. You'll literally just be paying them to look at your finances and give you advice.

Chapter 11: Create The Life You Want

When all is said and done, the whole point of you dumping your debt and building your bank is so that you can create the life that you want. That's a life that allows you to enjoy the present while also saving and preparing for the future.

In as much as your finances shouldn't be handled haphazardly, neither should your life. You should have a plan for what you want to achieve and how to achieve it. And though I'm sure you didn't come here for a life coaching session, you've probably already figured out that money is about more than just money.

The way that you manage money is just a physical manifestation of the things that are happening internally. If your life is a mess in other areas, it's inevitable that your money will be too. So, just like we started with mind work, let's finish it the same way.

In this final section of the book, I'll walk you through a process to help you define and accomplish your goals. Be it financial, career, or otherwise, these same steps will allow you to clearly define what it is that you want and the practical steps necessary to reach them.

If you really want to dive into this aspect of the book, you can check out the accompanying Goal Getter's Guide Workbook that's accessible in the Everyday Chick's Guide to Money digital workbook.

Creating Goals For Your Life & Your Finances

There are four primary phases to achieving any goal. Each is necessary to successfully reach every goal that you set for yourself.

Phase 1: Evaluation

Evaluating where you are today is the first phase to accomplishing any goals. You have to know where you are to determine the route to where you're going. Continual self-evaluation is the single most important thing that you can do to maintain a life of progression.

The most significant changes in my life were initiated by self-reflection. It came from facing the reality that I wasn't where I wanted to be and ultimately having the courage to make the change.

Take some time to reflect on your life—your faith, your finances, your health, relationships—the whole gambit. Are you where you want to be? You won't know until you evaluate your life.

Phase 2: Identification

This second phase is identifying and defining where you want to be. Without an end destination you'll continue to wander aimlessly through life. You have to know where you want to go.

What do you want your life to look like a year from now? What about five or ten years from now? What do you want your legacy to be? How do you want to be remembered?

Identify what you want your future self to look like. Create a vision for your future life so that you can create a plan to become it.

Phase 3: Preparation

The third phase is simply figuring out how you can take yourself from where you are to where you want to be. This is done through effectively planning.

Goals don't happen without a plan. Your plan is your preparation for the life that you'd like to create. It is the bridge from your current reality to your future.

Develop goals that are a B.R.I.D.G.E.—brief, realistic, incremental, detailed, gaugeable, executed. This is an acronym that I coined to share the six elements that are needed to accomplish your goals quickly and consistently. The BRIDGE will take you from a big picture plan to smaller, specific, actionable steps that you'll need to get to your final destination.

Phase 4: Manifestation

Manifestation isn't merely you accomplishing your goals. It is, within itself, a process. One consisting of perceiving, believing, and conceiving.

There's an old adage that goes, "Perception is reality." In the journey of attaining your goals, this couldn't be truer. Whatever you perceive, or see for yourself, you will manifest. If you see yourself as a failure, then don't be surprised when you fail.

There are two primary ways that you can alter your perception: exposure and visualization.

Exposure is simply putting yourself in environments that give you insight—or an insider's view—of the level you're trying to attain. An example is visiting homes in affluent neighborhoods to expose yourself to a higher standard of living. One form of exposure that I do occasionally is window shopping in luxury stores. Not only do I get to see and feel what luxury goods are like, but I begin to adopt the behaviors and thoughts of money of those who can afford to shop there.

Think about the ways that you will expose yourself to the level/goal that you are trying to attain.

Visualization happens when you condition your mind to imagine. The root word of imagine is "image." This means, you need to allow your mind to develop images of what you aspire to be or have. If your goal is to land your dream job, close your eyes and allow your mind to see images of you in your new office or sending off that email with your new title in the signature line. If your goal is to own a home, see yourself in the kitchen putting away dishes.

Set aside 10-15 mins in your day to do some intentional visualization. Begin your visualization exercise by clearing your mind and then focusing on what it is you desire. Engross yourself in the experience.

Next, create a vision board that you can see each day. Your vision board can be comprised of pictures and quotes that will trigger the vision of what you would like to accomplish. You can always use Pinterest as a digital form of your vision board.

The next step in manifesting your goals is believing that you can accomplish them. It is the assurance that what you desire to accomplish will be.

We have the ability to choose what we believe. If we didn't, there would only be such things as "truths," not beliefs. Therefore, you can choose to believe that you will accomplish your goals or not.

Your faith is based on a belief. You believe that the tenets of your faith are true, else you wouldn't practice it. In the same manner, if you believe that you can accomplish your goals, then you would do the necessary practices to operate under that premise.

Lastly, there is conception. Once you've perceived what you want to accomplish and believe that you can accomplish it, you must conceive it. This means putting in the work and taking daily steps to walk out the plan that you've created to reach your goals.

If you continue to follow this process for achieving your goals, nothing will be impossible for you.

A Final Note

I'm so excited that you have taken the steps necessary to dumping debt, building bank, and creating the life that you want. It is my prayer that everything outlined in this book will lead you to a life of financial freedom and happiness.

I don't want this to be the end of our journey together. I invite you to be a part of my private community of women from all over the world who are on the same journey as you. Just visit GirlTalkwithFo.com/VIP to join us!

ABOUT THE AUTHOR

Faneisha "Fo" Alexander is a Millennial personal finance expert whose story of paying off nearly $78,000 in debt in less than 3 years took the Internet by storm.

She is the editor and chief of the Girl Talk with Fo blog, a personal finance platform created to teach women how to dump debt, build bank, and create the life they want. Through her online platforms, she shares daily personal finance tips to help women begin to take control of their finances and, ultimately, their lives.

Fo is the former Miss Black South Carolina 2013, using her platform to promote financial literacy in underserved communities. She is a wife, author, entrepreneur, and host of the Girl Talk with Fo podcast—which is available on all podcast listening platforms. Her mission is to use her life's experiences to help others avoid their own financial pitfalls.

STAY CONNECTED!

Visit the website at *www.GirlTalkwithFo.com*.

Follow Faneisha on social media at @GirlTalkwithFo on Facebook, Instagram, Pinterest, and Twitter.

53854662R00083

Made in the USA
Columbia, SC
25 March 2019